Cordon Bleu

Meat Cookery

Cordon Bleu

Meat Cookery

SPHERE BOOKS LIMITED
30/32 Grays Inn Road, London, WC1X 8JL

First published in Great Britain in 1972 by
B.P.C. Publishing Ltd.

First Sphere edition 1973

Designed by Melvyn Kyte
Printed by Proost, Turnhout, Belgium

ISBN 0 7221 2510 0

These recipes have been adapted from the Cordon Bleu Cookery Course published by Purnell in association with the London Cordon Bleu Cookery School
Principal : Rosemary Hume ; Co-Principal : Muriel Downes
Quantities given are for 4 servings.
Spoon measures are level unless otherwise stated.

Contents

Introduction

Meat cookery is one of the most important parts of home management. For most families it is the prime source of protein in the diet; the butcher's bill takes a large proportion of the housekeeping each week, and whenever there is even a minor celebration, a good roast joint or a special braised dish is likely to be the centre of attraction.

Two things are therefore important for the Cordon Bleu cook : careful buying and expert preparation. This book is designed to help you with both these points. The section on meat management will help you plan what meat you want, and we have also given you some guidance on what to look for in a good cut of meat. Don't forget, though, that your butcher is the best judge of the meat he has in stock and you will be wise to ask his advice.

After that, the choice is yours and we have tried to include in this book as many methods of cooking as we could. Whether you choose a plain roast for the Sunday lunch, or a more elaborate one for a dinner party ; whether you decide to cook long and slow in the oven, or fast under the grill or in the sauté pan will depend on you, on your family's tastes and on what time you have.

Rosemary Hume
Muriel Downes

Roasting and accompaniments

Roasting is the traditional — and most popular — method of cooking in this country, so it is up to every serious student of cookery to master this most important art. Roasting embodies all that is best in English food: first-class meat plainly cooked, with vegetables, sauce and rich gravy served separately.

True roasting was always done on a revolving spit over an open fire. Only recently, however, has this become a practical reality in the home. Gas-fired and electric spits are now combined with the grill on many domestic cookers, or can be bought as separate units.

If you are not lucky enough to own a spit, you can obtain equally good results by roasting the meat in the oven. But, extra care is needed because cooking in the oven is really baking. The best procedure is as follows:

1 Remove the meat from the refrigerator 30 minutes before cooking — meat should be at room temperature before being placed in a hot oven.

2 Pre-heat the oven to the correct temperature, first checking that the shelf is in position and will take the joint comfortably. The correct position varies with the type of oven, so do follow the manufacturer's instructions carefully.

3 Put the roasting tin in the oven with 2-3 tablespoons of dripping, depending on the size of the joint.

4 When the dripping is smoking, set the meat on a grid or simply on the bottom of the tin. Baste well to seal in the juices and return to the oven. If you are not using a grid, place the joint on its edge rather than flat on the outside, since the part in contact with the tin may get hard and overcook. This is especially important with a round joint, eg. sirloin.

5 Cook according to the weight and thickness of the joint (see chart, page 11), basting every 15-20 minutes to keep the meat moist and tender until done.

6 Once the meat is cooked, it should be dished up and placed in the warming drawer of the cooker. Plan the cooking time to allow the meat to stand for 15 minutes while the gravy is prepared and vegetables dished up. This standing time will make the meat much easier to carve.

7 A roast joint needs good gravy: strong and clear for beef, mutton and lamb, and lightly thickened for pork and veal. Serve gravy separately in a gravy boat.

Gravy

The basis of gravy is, of course, the meat's sediment and juices left in the roasting tin. To increase the amount, add stock. For mutton and lamb, simmer the knuckle bone from the leg or shoulder (or the chine bone from the loin) with water and vegetables to flavour. For a joint of beef, when no bone or stock is available, potato water or a bouillon cube can be used, but be sparing with seasoning since both can be salty.

When the meat is dished up, tilt the roasting tin gently to pour off the fat, but keep back the juices and sediment from the meat. Dust in just enough flour to absorb the small quantity of dripping left in the roasting tin (not usually more than 1 dessertspoon of flour for beef or lamb). Allow to colour very slowly, then scrape tin well to take up the sediment round the sides.

Pour on $\frac{1}{2}$-$\frac{3}{4}$ pint stock, bring to the boil and season with salt and pepper. Reduce the quantity to concentrate the flavour. If necessary, you can improve the colour with a little gravy browning. This is better than scorching the flour in a thin roasting tin. Strain into a gravy boat. Serve very hot.

Roasting times for meat

	Oven temperature	Total cooking time (equal for gas and electricity)	
Beef	Electric oven 375° F Gas Mark 7 for the first 15 minutes then reduce to Mark 6	Rare : Well done :	15 minutes per lb and 15 minutes over 20 minutes per lb and 30 minutes over Since the cooking time varies with the thickness of the joint and not always according to the weight, allow : 45 minutes for joints under $1\frac{1}{2}$ lb $1\frac{1}{4}$ hours for joints under 3 lb
Lamb	Electric oven 375° F Gas Mark 6		20 minutes per lb and 20 minutes over
Mutton	Electric oven 375° F Gas Mark 6 for the first 15 minutes, then reduce to Mark 5		20 minutes per lb and 20 minutes over
Pork	Electric oven 375° F Gas Mark 7 for the first 15 minutes, then reduce to Mark 6		25 minutes per lb and 25 minutes over

The electricity settings and gas Marks given here are not always comparable because an electric oven, being entirely enclosed, gives a constant heat all over, whereas a gas oven, with its open flue, has 3 different heat zones.

Beef cuts for roasting

When beef is well hung, as it should be, it is purplish-red in colour. Beef that is too fresh and bright red improves if kept in refrigerator for a few days before cooking. Fat should be creamy in colour. In prime cuts, like sirloin, there is a light marbling of fat through lean meat. Fat helps to keep a joint tender, so make sure its natural fat is adhering and not an extra slab which has been tied on by the butcher. Accompaniments for roast beef are given on pages 14-17. For roasting times, see previous page, and pages 22-24 for slow and spit roasting.

Sirloin

The joint should weigh not less than 3½-4 lb on the bone and contain the undercut or fillet. It can be boned and rolled, although meat is juicier and has more flavour when roasted on the bone. Butchers often bone and roll sirloin in order to make smaller joints from this prime cut. Continental butchers offer contrefilet, or entrecôte, a compact joint from the top of the sirloin. It is always well trimmed, free of bone and excess fat, so it is expensive.

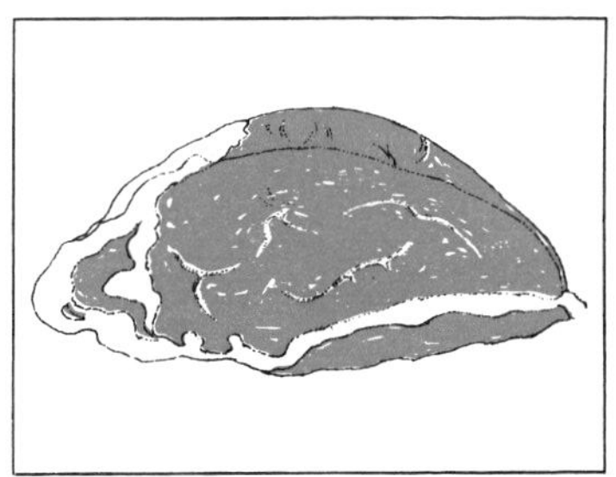

Fillet

An excellent joint for a party or the cold table, fillet is the undercut from the sirloin which can extend into the rump (rump fillet). It has little or no fat and so is frequently larded (ie. wrapped round with pork fat, or larding bacon, which can, alternatively, be sewn in the surface of the joint with a larding needle).

Since fillet is a small joint of 2 lb and upwards, it must have a fierce oven and be roasted on a grid. It is very tender meat.

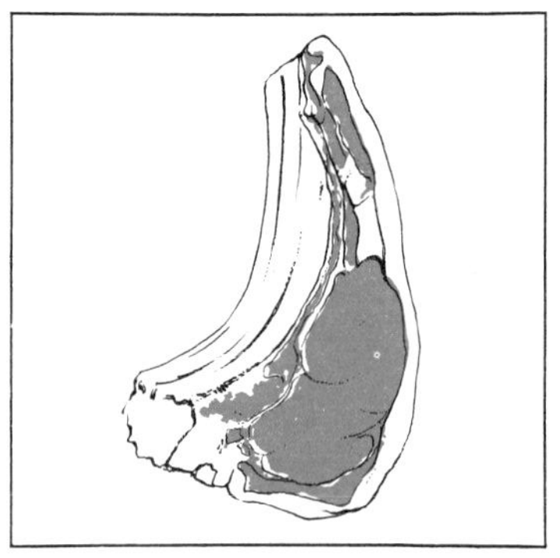

Rib roast and wing rib

Large joints of 4-5 lb and upwards. Like sirloin, these can be boned and rolled.

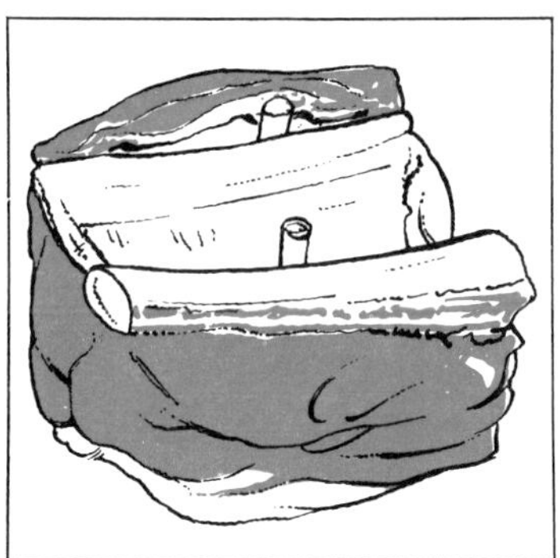

Top ribs, or Jacob's ladder

This joint is called Jacob's ladder because the lean meat and fat layers on top of the bone make it rise during cooking and so resemble the rungs of a ladder. If you like fat, you will like Jacob's ladder, and this joint is excellent eaten cold.

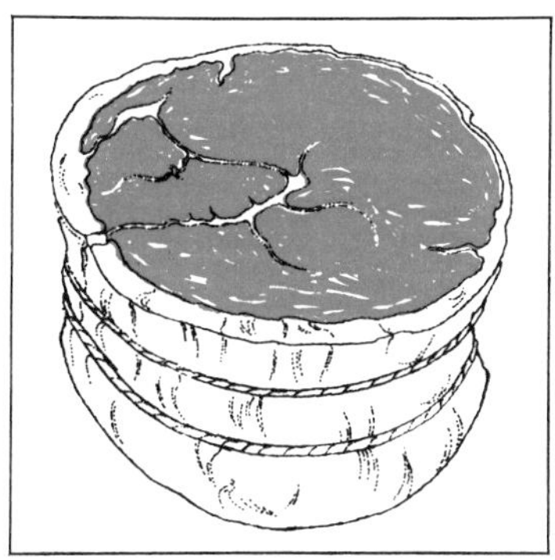

Topside

Although sold as a roasting joint, topside is really better braised or pot roasted. If roasted, it must be left rare or underdone to keep it tender because the meat is exceptionally lean. Overcooking makes this cut dry and hard. Small joints of 1 ½ lb and upwards can be cut from topside.

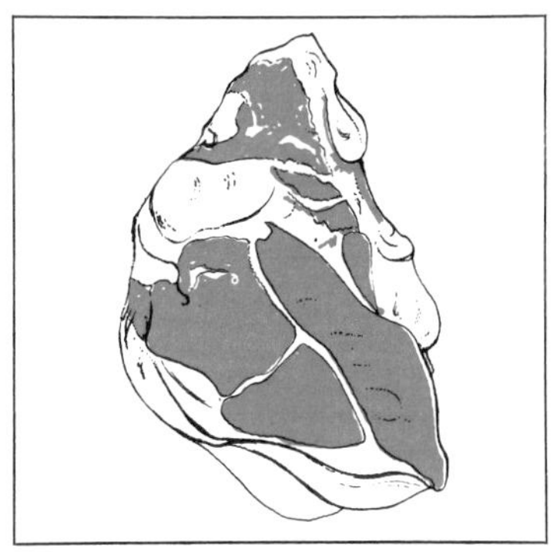

Aitchbone

This is a very large joint rarely cut these days, lying between the rump, topside and silverside. On the bone (pelvic) it weighs about 12 lb, but nowadays butchers usually remove the bone and cut roughly triangular shaped joints from this section that weigh 2½ - 4½ lb. The meat has a good flavour and is tender. At the apex it is fine-grained with natural fat adhering. At the base the meat is lean and rather coarse-grained, so it is better under-roasted.

Accompaniments to beef roasts

Yorkshire pudding

5 oz plain flour
pinch of salt
1 large egg
½ pint milk and water mixed ¾ milk to ¼ water)
1 tablespoon dripping
1 tablespoon beef suet (finely grated) — optional

Method

Sift the flour with the salt into a mixing bowl. Make a well in the centre and put in the unbeaten egg and half the milk and water. Stir carefully, gradually drawing in the flour. Add half the remaining milk and water and beat well. Stir in the rest of the liquid and leave in a cool place for about 1 hour before cooking.

Set the oven at 400-450°F or Mark 7.

Heat the dripping in a shallow dish until hot (a tin or enamel dish is most satisfactory). Tilt the dish round to coat sides with the hot dripping. Then pour in the batter. Bake for 30-40 minutes in the pre-set hot oven on a shelf well above the meat.

This recipe gives a light, well-risen pudding. If you prefer something more substantial, stir 1 tablespoon beef suet (finely grated) into the mixture before baking.

The basic ingredients that go to make up Yorkshire pudding, without which many would consider Sunday's roast beef incomplete

Baked (roast) potatoes

Choose medium to large potatoes of even size. Peel and blanch by putting into cold salted water and bringing to the boil. Drain thoroughly and lightly scratch the surface with a fork (this will prevent a dry and leathery exterior after cooking). Now put the potatoes into hot fat in the same tin as the meat, 40-45 minutes before the meat is fully cooked, and baste well. Cook until soft (test by piercing with a cooking fork or fine skewer), basting them when you baste the meat and turning after 25 minutes. Drain well on kitchen paper, pile in a vegetable dish and sprinkle with a little salt. Do not cover before serving.

Buttered marrow

1 marrow
1-2 oz butter
salt and pepper
parsley (chopped)

Method

Peel the marrow, remove seeds and cut into 2-inch squares. Melt butter in a large shallow pan and add marrow. Season and cover with buttered paper and a lid. Cook over gentle heat until tender, shaking the pan from time to time. Allow 15-20 minutes cooking time and garnish with chopped parsley.

Cabbage

The most English — and most maligned — of all vegetables. To overcome this reputation every Cordon Bleu cook must remember the following golden rules :

1 Cabbage, like all vegetables that grow above the ground, must be put into plenty of boiling salted water and cooked uncovered.

2 Remove coarser outer leaves. Do not make a cut in stem base because this will spoil the shape and allow juices to escape. Wash well in several waters.

3 Avoid overcooking. For plain boiling, 10-12 minutes is enough. Although the cabbage must be tender, it should still have a certain bite and crispness. After draining, finish cooking in butter.

4 Avoid keeping cabbage hot for any length of time because this will give it an unpleasant smell and spoil the colour. Cook it early, by all means, but when tender tip into a colander, drain and rinse well with cold water. This will set the bright green colour. When the meal is nearly ready, turn the cabbage into a large shallow pan, heat quickly until steam stops rising, then add $\frac{1}{2}$-1 oz butter in small pieces and toss until melted. Season and serve.

Accompaniments to beef roasts

continued

Glazed carrots

1-2 lb carrots
1 teaspoon granulated sugar
1 oz butter
salt
mint (chopped)

Method

Peel carrots and, if small, leave them whole or quarter them ; if very large, cut in thin slices. Put in a pan with water to cover, sugar, butter and a pinch of salt. Cover and cook steadily until tender, then remove lid and cook until all the water has evaporated, when the butter and sugar will form a glaze round the carrots.

Add a little chopped mint just before serving.

Creamed swedes

These should not be dismissed as something nasty remembered from schooldays. Try swedes this way and give them a chance.

1 lb swedes
1 oz butter
black pepper
1 small carton ($2\frac{1}{2}$ fl oz) double cream

Method

Peel swedes, cut into even-size wedges and cook in salted water until tender. Drain well and return to the heat to dry. Crush with a potato masher or fork, add the butter and continue cooking over gentle heat until all the water has gone. Season and pour in the cream just before serving the swedes.

Horseradish cream

2 tablespoons freshly grated horseradish
1 dessertspoon white wine vinegar
1 teaspoon dry mustard
1 rounded teaspoon caster sugar
pinch of salt
black pepper (ground from mill)
1 small carton ($2\frac{1}{2}$ fl oz) double cream

Method

Mix the vinegar and seasonings together and add the horseradish. Lightly whip the cream and mix gently into the other ingredients.

When fresh horseradish is unobtainable, use grated horseradish preserved in vinegar and mix the seasoning with only 1 teaspoon of vinegar.

There's nothing quite like a tender joint of roast beef, slightly pink in the centre, with baked (roast) potatoes and Yorkshire pudding

Roast fillet of beef Dubarry

$2\frac{1}{2}$-3 lb fillet of beef
piece of pork fat, or unsmoked bacon fat, or beef fat (for barding)
2-3 tablespoons oil, or beef dripping

For gravy
1 dessertspoon plain flour
$\frac{1}{2}$-$\frac{3}{4}$ pint beef stock (see page 155)
salt and pepper

For garnish
1 large cauliflower
little grated cheese

For thick mornay sauce
1 oz butter
2 tablespoons plain flour
1 pint milk
2 oz grated cheese

Method

The garnish can be prepared ahead of time. Break the cauliflower into sprigs and cook until just tender in boiling, salted water (about 5 minutes). Drain and refresh by pouring over cold water. Press 1-2 cauliflower sprigs at a time in muslin to form balls and set them on a buttered baking sheet. Prepare a thick mornay sauce (see page 154), and coat the tiny cauliflower sprigs with this. Sprinkle with a little extra grated cheese and keep on one side.

Bard (wrap fat round) meat and tie at regular intervals with fine string. The pork fat protects the very lean meat and keeps it moist during cooking. If you do not like the flavour of pork or bacon fat, put an extra piece of beef fat on top of the meat after it has been tied with string. The string keeps the meat in good shape while cooking; without it small pieces of fillet curl when first basted and put in the oven.

Set oven at 400°F or Mark 7. Heat oil or dripping in roasting tin and when hot, take out of oven, put in the fillet, baste, turn and baste again. Lift joint on to grill pan grid, or place on a wire cake rack, and stand this in the roasting tin. (This prevents the sides and bottom of the joint coming in contact with the tin, which would harden and spoil this lean meat.) Baste every 15 minutes and turn when half cooked.

If using a gas oven, allow 15 minutes per lb and 15 minutes over for a 2 lb joint, or 15 minutes per lb with no extra time for a 3 lb or larger piece.

If using an electric oven, allow only 10 minutes per lb, with no extra time. Then remove meat, turn oven off, place on a fireproof dish and return to the oven to finish cooking in the residual heat for up to 30 minutes.

Take cooked meat from oven, remove string and barding fat; keep joint warm. Prepare the gravy (see page 10) and strain into a gravy boat.

Just before serving, carve the meat in the kitchen and put back on the hot serving dish, spooning any juice that runs out over the meat.

Watchpoint Never add these juices to the gravy as they would coagulate and spoil its appearance.

Arrange the small cauliflower sprigs around the dish and serve potatoes separately.

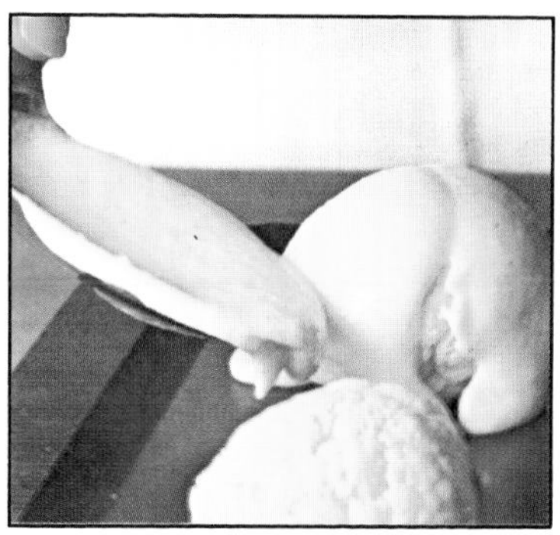

The garnish for fillet of beef is prepared by pressing together cauliflower sprigs (a few at a time) in a piece of muslin to form balls. The cauliflower balls are placed on a greased baking sheet. Mornay sauce is then spooned over each one and the whole is sprinkled with grated cheese ready for baking in oven. Below : the finished dish

Fillet of beef niçoise

1½ lb fillet of beef
piece of pork fat, or unsmoked bacon fat, or beef fat (for barding)
2-3 tablespoons olive oil (for roasting)
1 pint aspic jelly

For salad
1 large aubergine
4 tablespoons olive oil
1 onion (sliced)
2 green peppers (cored, shredded and blanched)
salt and pepper
1 lb tomatoes (skinned, quartered and seeds removed)
2-3 tablespoons French dressing (see page 153)

For cream dressing
1 clove of garlic (crushed with a little salt)
1 teaspoon paprika pepper
1 large carton (5 fl oz) of soured, or cultured, cream
pepper (ground from mill)
lemon juice, or wine vinegar (to taste)

For garnish
3 eggs (hard-boiled and quartered, or sliced)
2 oz black olives (stoned)

This quantity serves 10-12 people.

Aspic jelly can be made with powdered aspic, with a glass of sherry (2½ fl oz) replacing the equivalent of water.

Method

Bard the fillet of beef and roast in the oven at 400°F or Mark 7 for about 35 minutes (see method, page 18). Leave to cool.

Slice the aubergine, score the cut surface with a knife, sprinkle with, salt and leave it for 20-30 minutes, then drain off liquid.

Heat the oil in a frying pan and lightly fry aubergine slices on both sides. Reduce the heat, add the onion to the pan and continue cooking until it is soft but not coloured, then add the peppers and seasoning and cook for 2-3 minutes when the aubergine should be tender. Increase the heat under the pan, add the tomatoes and cook briskly for 1 minute. Turn salad into a dish, leave to cool, then moisten with French dressing.

To prepare the cream dressing: work the crushed garlic and paprika into the soured (or cultured) cream. Season with pepper and add the lemon juice (or wine vinegar) to taste.

Carve the beef, arrange in overlapping slices round a flat serving dish. Brush well with cool aspic jelly, giving 2-3 coats, and leave to set. Spoon salad into centre of dish and garnish with eggs and olives. Serve dressing and hot anchovy loaf separately.

Frying the aubergine and onion slices lightly in oil on both sides

Basting the cold slices of roast beef with 2-3 coats of cool aspic jelly, allowing each one to set before adding the next

Hot anchovy loaf

Set oven at 400°F or Mark 6. Soak 6 anchovy fillets in a little milk, then drain and chop. Pound with 3-4 oz unsalted butter and add enough anchovy essence to flavour well and colour the butter a delicate pink. Season with pepper.

Slice a French loaf evenly down to crust, but not right through. Spread anchovy butter between slices and on top and sides of loaf. Wrap in foil and bake in oven until crisp and golden-brown (about 20 minutes). Remove foil, serve loaf hot — keep it whole so that guests can break off a slice as wanted.

Slow and spit roasting

Through research into providing food at budget cost, it has been discovered that there is much less shrinkage if meat is slow roasted (the oven is set at 350°F or Mark 4 for pork, and at 325°F or Mark 3 for all other meats) ; and now that beef particularly is so expensive it is worthwhile for the housewife to experiment with this method and to benefit from the information obtained.

When slow roasting, the only way to ensure that the meat is fully cooked in the centre is to use a meat thermometer. The chart (see right) gives an approximate time per lb for the various joints of meat (assuming them to be taken straight out of the refrigerator), and the temperatures your thermometer must register.

Remember the thermometer must be inserted into the thickest part of the meat and must never touch the bone, nor rest on the fat, and that the times given may vary with the size and shape of the joint, and also the amount of fat.

Joints on the bone must always be set on a rack, fat side uppermost, in the roasting tin. It is not necessary to add extra fat, nor is it necessary to baste. Boned and rolled joints, or those cut from boneless meat, should be spread with a little good dripping and set on a rack in the tin in the same way. There is no need to baste, but they should be turned half way through the cooking.

It is now possible for many more people to spit roast at home, and electrically operated rotating spits do give an almost exact copy of the old spit roast before an open fire. This method is more like slow roasting, the shrinkage is less, and the flavour is particularly fine as the outside fat develops such a good flavour. In fact, we feel that this is the only way to roast a joint of topside, a small lean joint which tends to become hard on the outside when ovenroasted.

It is important that meat to be spit roasted is at room temperature, so remove it from the refrigerator 1-2 hours before cooking.

Joints with a cut surface are cooked on very high heat until the meat just begins to take colour. The heat should then be turned quite low (each cooker will have its own instructions in the handbook), and the meat is cooked at black heat (ie. not radiant heat) until it is tender. Follow the timing given in the chart (see right). Brush or baste the joint with dripping from time to time during the cooking.

Spit roasting guide

Beef

The cut surface of the joint must always be exposed to the heat in order to seal it and retain the juices. In a joint of wing rib or sirloin the spit should be inserted in such a position that it does not touch the bone, so that the fat and both sides of the lean of the meat are exposed in turn as the joint rotates. If the spit touches the bone it upsets the distribution of heat or may stop it altogether.

SLOW ROASTING CHART

Set oven at 350°F or Mark 4 for pork, and 325°F or Mark 3 for other meat

Cuts of meat (taken straight from refrigerator)	Approximate time per lb for 3-6 lb joints	Temperature on meat thermometer
Beef on the bone		
sirloin — rare	26	140°F
wing rib — medium	30	160°F
rib roast — well done	35	170°F
Lamb		
leg	35-40	175°F-182°F
neck, best end and loin	45	182°F
shoulder	35	182°F
shoulder, boned and rolled	55	182°F
Pork		
leg	45-50	185°F
loin	35-40	185°F
shoulder, a joint from the blade	40-50	185°F
shoulder, boned and rolled	55	185°F
Veal		
leg	35-40	180°F
loin	35-40	180°F
shoulder, boneless roll	55	180°F

SPIT ROASTING CHART

	Minutes per lb
Beef	
without bone	10-25
with bone	20-25
Lamb	25-35
Pork	30-35
Hares and rabbits	
stuffed	20-25
unstuffed	15
Poultry	
stuffed	20-25
unstuffed	15-20

Slow and spit roasting

Lamb

A leg of lamb can be spit roasted but particular care must be taken in inserting the spit because of the position of the bone.

A shoulder of lamb should be fully or partially boned.

Pork

Joints cut from the leg should be boned and stuffed, but remember that the stuffing will swell, so it is wise to put in only the very minimum amount and secure it well by sewing up with a trussing needle and thread. Extra stuffing can always be made and cooked separately. Shoulder cuts, providing they have been removed from the bone, are suitable for spit roasting, but a whole leg would be too large.

Gravy for spit roasted joints

The making of a good gravy is something of a problem when spit roasting because although the drip tray will have collected a certain amount of juice and quite a lot of fat during the cooking time, the tin itself is not suitable for making gravy.

Any juices that fall from the meat, congeal and then brown on the drip tray must be carefully scooped up, added to a little good stock and then boiled up well. If the family likes plenty of gravy, this can be augmented by adding potato water, if there is no stock, and gravy salt for colouring and flavour. It can be thickened too, if liked.

Lamb cuts for roasting

The size of the carcass varies with the breed of lamb, but the best is small with a reasonable covering of firm white fat. The meat is pale to dark red in colour. As with beef, lamb tastes better if it has been hung. It should not be served underdone, but should have just a tinge of pink at the centre. Mint sauce is traditionally served with lamb. Other accompaniments are given on page 28. For roasting times see pages 11 and 23.

Crown roast

Ask your butcher to prepare this joint, which is good for dinner parties of 6-8 people. Its crown shape is achieved by turning outwards two best ends of neck, which are then trussed and skewered together to form a circle. The centre of this roast may be stuffed or filled with spring vegetables before serving. Crown the top bones with cutlet frills.

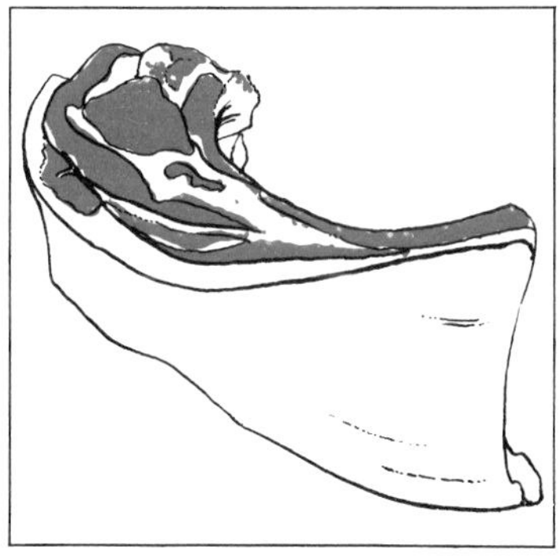

Best end of neck

An excellent small joint for 3-4 people, the whole best end consists of 6-7 cutlet bones and weighs $1\frac{1}{2}$-2 lb. The joint should be chined and the bones sawn through 2-3 inches from the top.

To prepare neck for roasting: first, cut away the chine bone (half backbone) and keep for making gravy. Then cut off the flap containing the top of the cutlet bones and keep for roasting with the neck — but cut into pieces before serving. The fat from the top of the bones should be sliced away to a depth of $1\frac{1}{2}$-2 inches. Cut away gristly meat between the cleared bones with a small knife and scrape bone clean. Be sure to skin the fat side of the neck (if not already done by the butcher) and score in a lattice pattern with the point of the knife.

Lamb cuts for roasting continued

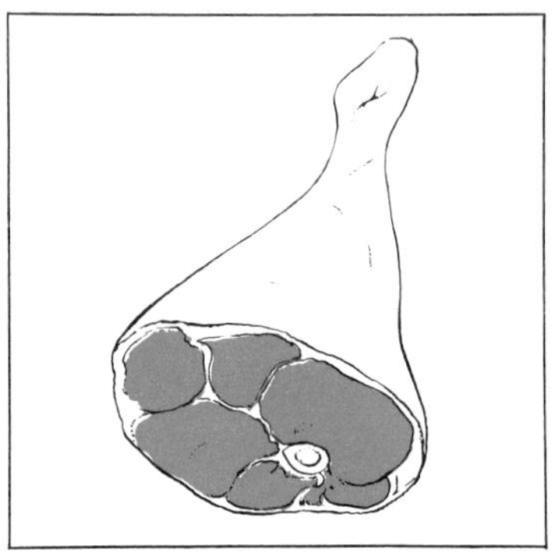

Leg

This is the leanest cut so it needs to be well basted during roasting. The weight varies from 3-5 lb, and the largest legs are frequently halved and sold as shank and fillet end.

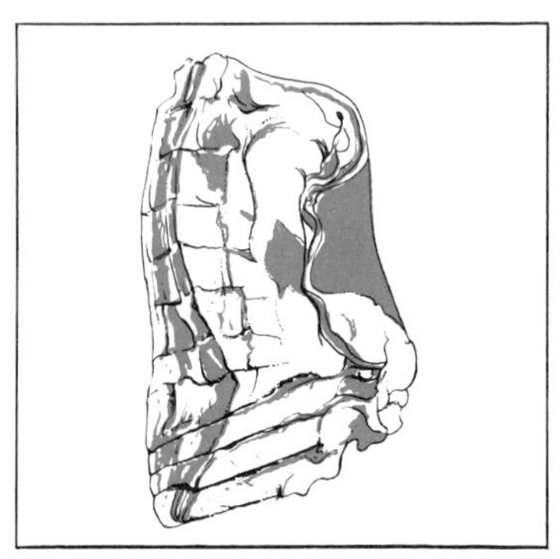

Loin

Loin is very sweet meat. It is rather wasteful because of a generous amount of fat on the underside. Carving is easier if the joint is chined, not chopped, by the butcher. It is good when boned and stuffed.

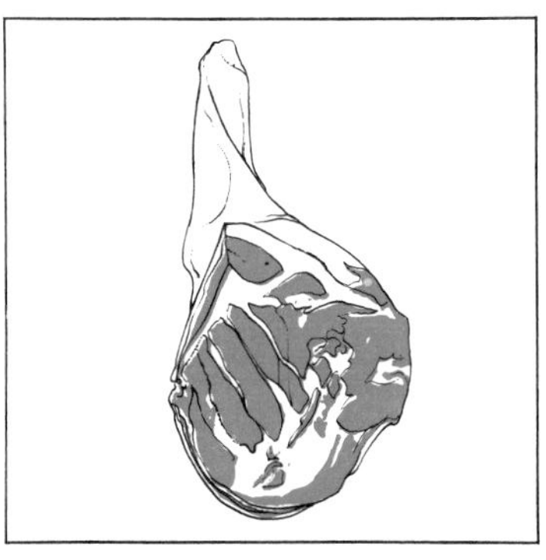

Shoulder

Particularly well flavoured and juicy, shoulder has a good proportion of fat to lean. It is equally good roasted plain, or boned and stuffed.

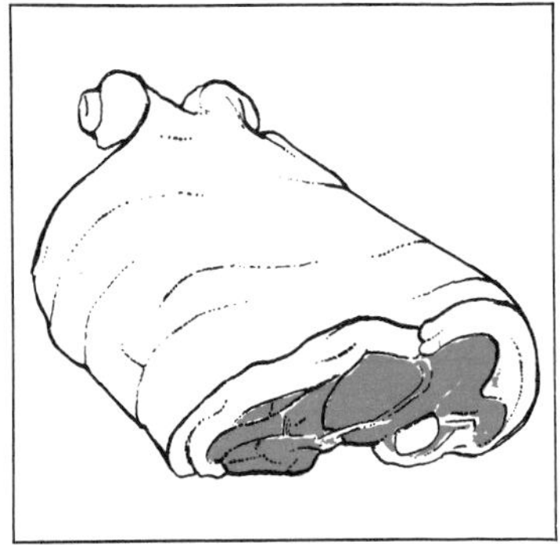

Saddle

The joint for a big party or special occasion, saddle is the double loin taken from the top end down to the tail and corresponds to a baron of beef. Its weight averages 8-10 lb and this will serve 8-10 people.

One of the more economical cuts of lamb, a best end of neck should be well trimmed and scored. Cut into cutlets for serving

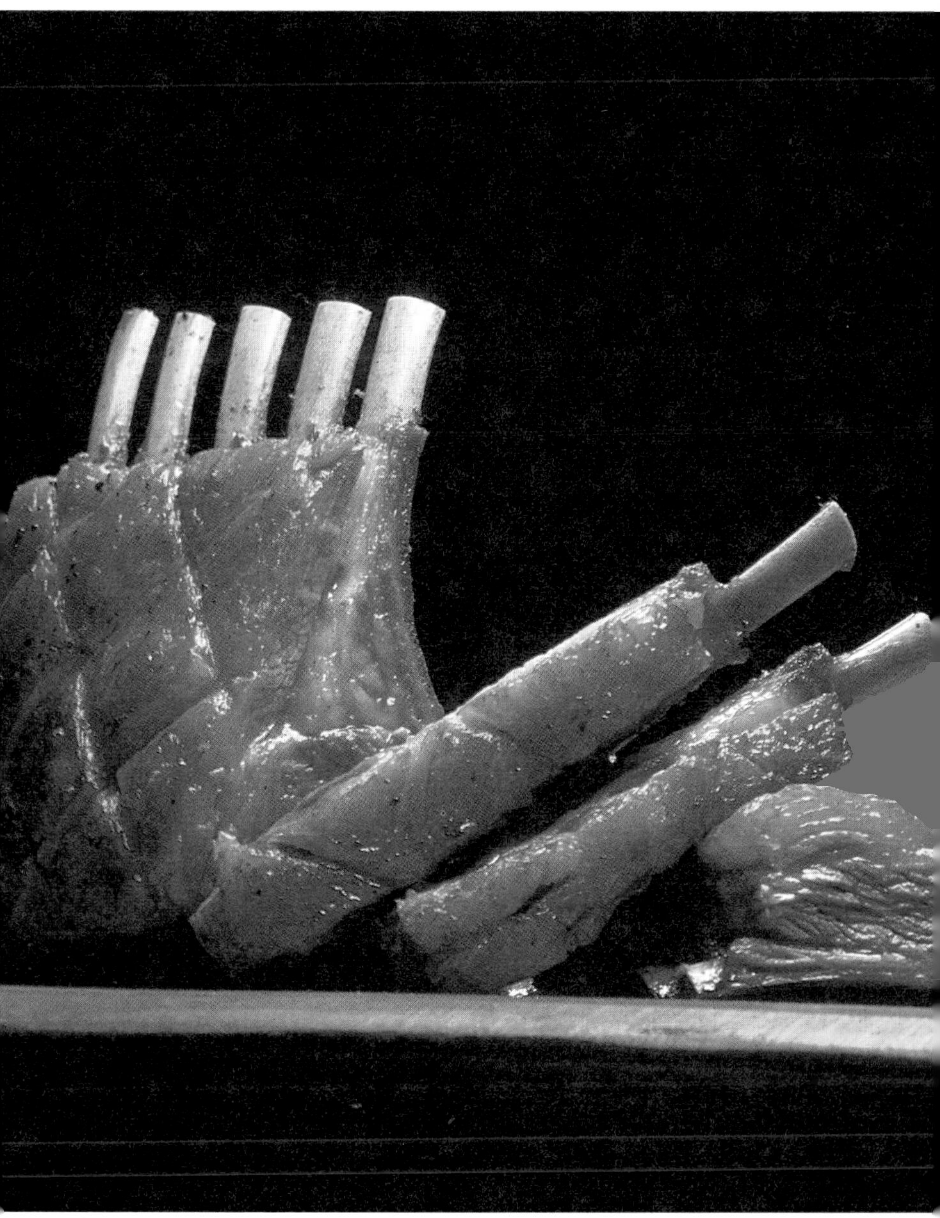

Accompaniments to lamb roasts

Mint sauce

2 tablespoons fresh mint
1-2 tablespoons caster sugar
wine vinegar (to taste)

Method

Mint sauce should be bright green, smooth and pulpy in consistency. Chop the mint and pound with a little of the caster sugar until quite smooth. Add 1-2 tablespoons boiling water, according to the quantity of mint, to improve the colour and melt the sugar. Add a little wine vinegar to taste.

Boulangère potatoes

1½ lb potatoes
3 medium-size onions
salt and pepper
¾ pint stock (see page 155)
1 bayleaf
1 tablespoon dripping

Method

Slice onions, blanch by putting in cold water, bring to the boil and boil for 1 minute before draining. Peel and slice potatoes in thin rounds and place immediately in an ovenproof dish layered with the onions, salt and pepper. Pour over just enough stock to cover and add bayleaf. Dot well with dripping and bake for 1 hour in an oven at 400°F or Mark 6 until tender and well browned.

To get the best results, remove from oven halfway through cooking time when, if top layer of potatoes has curled up, press down into the stock with basting spoon and add a little extra dripping, if necessary.

Vegetables

For those who insist on green peas with lamb all the year round, frozen peas are the answer. The A.F.D. (accelerated freeze dried) peas lend themselves to cooking à la française and can be very good. Fresh runner beans, brussels sprouts and spring greens (or jerusalem artichokes boiled or roasted round the meat) are all good with lamb.

Petits pois à la française

1 packet of A.F.D. peas
4 outside leaves of lettuce (finely shredded)
6 spring onions (cut in pieces)
kneaded butter (see below)

Method

Follow the cooking instructions on the packet of peas, adding the lettuce leaves and spring onions. When peas are tender, add just enough kneaded butter in small pieces to bind peas, lettuce and liquid together.

Kneaded butter (beurre manié)

This is a liaison for thickening. Work twice as much butter as flour into a paste on a plate with a fork, and add in small pieces to the cooled mixture off the heat. Stir, shake the pan and reboil. If still not thick enough, add more. You will find the butter melts and draws the flour into the liquid.

Mutton

Mutton is, technically, the carcass of an animal over 2 years old. It is always served well cooked and the loin or saddle is the best joint for roasting. Either onion sauce or redcurrant jelly go well with mutton.

Onion sauce

3 medium-size onions (sliced)
1 oz butter
2 tablespoons plain flour
½ pint milk
salt and pepper
1 tablespoon cream, or
½ oz butter (optional)

Method

Slice the onions and cook in boiling, salted water until tender. Drain thoroughly and sieve, or blend if you prefer a smooth sauce.

Melt the butter, take off the heat and add the flour. Tip on the scalded milk (scalding the milk will make it less likely to curdle) and, when thoroughly blended, stir continually over moderate heat until boiling. Simmer 2-3 minutes, add the prepared onions, adjust seasoning and finish with a spoonful of cream or a knob of butter.

Redcurrant jelly

It is not possible to give a specific quantity of redcurrants as the recipe is governed by the amount of juice made, which is variable.

Method

Wash the fruit and, without removing from the stems, put in a 7 lb jam jar or stone crock. Cover and stand in deep pan of hot water. Simmer on top of the stove or in the oven at 350°F or Mark 4, mashing the fruit a little from time to time, until all the juice is extracted (about 1 hour).

Then turn fruit into a jelly-bag, or double linen strainer, and allow to drain undisturbed overnight over a basin.

Watchpoint To keep the jelly clear and sparkling, do not try to speed up the draining process by forcing juice through ; this will only make the jelly cloudy.

Now measure juice. Allowing 1 lb lump or preserving sugar to each pint of juice, mix juice and sugar together, dissolving over slow heat. When dissolved, bring to the boil, boil hard for 3-5 minutes and skim with a wooden spoon. Test a little on a saucer : allow jelly to cool, tilt saucer and, if jelly is set, it will wrinkle. Put into jam jars, place small circles of greaseproof paper over jelly, label and cover with jam pot covers. Store in a dry larder until required.

Leg of lamb duxelles

1 small leg of lamb
2-3 oz butter
garlic slivers
1 wineglass white wine
stock (made with knuckle bone from lamb — see page 155)
little arrowroot (optional)
2 oz Parmesan cheese (grated)
watercress (to garnish)

For duxelles filling
$\frac{1}{2}$-$\frac{3}{4}$ lb mushrooms (finely chopped)
1 oz butter
2 shallots (finely chopped)
1 tablespoon chopped thyme
1 tablespoon chopped parsley
3 tablespoons white breadcrumbs (see page 152)
salt and pepper

Method

Rub the leg well with 1 oz of butter. Insert the garlic slivers, wrap in buttered paper, put in a roasting tin and pour the white wine round, reserving a little. Roast meat in the oven at 350 F or Mark 4, allowing 15-20 minutes per lb. When half done take off the paper; baste meat frequently until cooked. Remove meat from oven and cool slightly. Strain juice from pan, getting rid of excess fat. Deglaze pan with reserved wine and stock. Season, strain into juice. If you wish, thicken with a little arrowroot and set aside.

Prepare filling while lamb is roasting. Wash and chop the mushrooms finely, melt butter in pan, add shallots and 1 minute later mushrooms, followed by the herbs. Now cook briskly for 5-6 minutes, draw aside from heat before adding crumbs and seasoning.

Slice lamb and insert some of filling between each slice. Reshape leg before putting back into roasting tin. Work 2 oz of the butter with the same amount of cheese and spread all over the surface of the meat. Ten minutes before you serve the leg, put in a hot oven to brown.

Serve on a hot dish with a little of the gravy round and the rest in a gravy boat. Garnish with watercress.

If only the top part of the leg is sliced, there should be enough meat left on the underside to make a good 'réchauffé' (dish made from cooked food) for reheating on following day.

Glazed onions

Cover the onions with cold water, add salt and bring to the boil. Tip off the water, add 1-1$\frac{1}{2}$ oz butter and a dusting of caster sugar. Cover and cook gently until golden-brown on all sides, and cooked through (about 10 minutes).

Loin of lamb bretonne

2-3 lb loin of lamb (boned)
2-3 tablespoons dripping

For stuffing
2 tablespoons chopped onion
1 oz butter
5 tablespoons fresh white breadcrumbs
2 tablespoons chopped mixed herbs
grated rind and little juice of 1 organge
salt and pepper
seasoned flour
beaten egg
browned crumbs (see page 153)

For sauce
1 onion (sliced)
$\frac{1}{2}$ pint stock (made with the bones, 1 onion, 1 carrot and bouquet garni to flavour) — see page 155)
1-2 tablespoons redcurrant jelly (see page 29)
orange juice
12 glazed onions and several carrots (to garnish)

If not boned, ask the butcher to chine the loin, rather than chop it. Prepare the stuffing : cook the onion in the butter until soft but not coloured. Add it to the white crumbs with the herbs, orange rind and seasoning. Bind with the orange juice and a little beaten egg. Spread this over the inside of the meat, roll up and tie securely with string. Roll in seasoned flour, brush with beaten egg and roll in browned crumbs. Pre-set oven at 375°F or Mark 6.

Heat the dripping in a roasting tin and, when hot, put in the meat, baste and set to roast for $1\frac{1}{4}$-$1\frac{1}{2}$ hours. Prepare a good stock from the bones. When cooked, take up the meat, remove string and keep warm while you prepare the sauce. Tip off fat from the roasting tin, leaving the sediment in the bottom. Add the sliced onion and cook slowly until brown. Dust in a little flour, add the stock and redcurrant jelly, boil up well, season, sharpen with a little orange juice and then strain.

Carve the meat, arrange in a serving dish, garnish with glazed onions (opposite) and carrots (see page 16). Spoon over a little of the sauce and serve the rest separately.

Loin of lamb bretonne, with a garnish of glazed onions and carrots. Before roasting, the stuffed joint is rolled in a little seasoned flour, brushed with beaten egg and, finally, rolled more in browned breadcrumbs

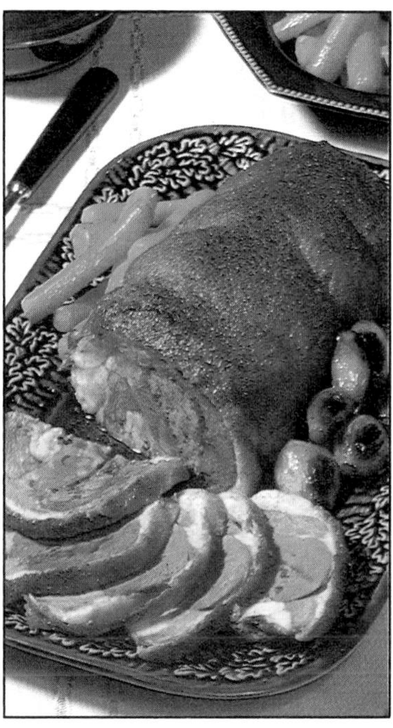

Noisettes of lamb papillon

2 lb best end of neck of lamb (boned out)
butter (for roasting)
1 wineglass white wine

For garnish
8-10 large flat mushrooms
1 oz butter

For sauce
2 shallots (finely chopped)
2 mushrooms (chopped)
$\frac{1}{2}$ oz butter
1 dessertspoon chopped mixed herbs, or parsley
1 wineglass white wine
1 teaspoon plain flour
$\frac{1}{4}$ pint stock (see page 155)

Method

Roll up the lamb and tie securely with fine string. Spread with butter, place lamb in a roasting tin and pour over wine. Roast for about $1\frac{1}{4}$ hours, basting well, in the oven at 375°F or Mark 5, or on spit (20 minutes per lb and 20 minutes over).

Meanwhile peel and trim the mushrooms for garnish (reserving trimmings); fry quickly in a little butter. Keep warm.

To prepare sauce: cook the shallots, chopped mushrooms and reserved trimmings in butter for 1-2 minutes. Add the herbs and wine, boil to reduce a little and set aside.

Take up the lamb, pour off any fat, add the flour to the tin and moisten with the stock. Boil to reduce a little and strain on to the mushroom and shallot mixture. Season and simmer for a few minutes.

Cut the lamb in $\frac{1}{2}$ - $\frac{3}{4}$ inch slices, dish up 'en couronne', setting a mushroom between each slice. Pour the sauce over and garnish the centre of the dish with parisienne potatoes (see page 80).

Cutlets '**en couronne**' are arranged in a circle overlapping round the outside of the dish, with the bones upwards, and the garnish then placed in the centre. To prevent the cutlets from slipping, a small quantity of sauce can be placed on the dish to secure them.

Pork cuts for roasting

The flesh of pork should be firm, the lean pinkish-white, and the fat white and smooth. The skin of the hindquarter gives the best crackling and both skin and rind should be thin and supple. Pork must always be well cooked to prevent the danger of infection which may be present in the meat. Any juices that run through the meat after cooking should be clear — not pink, which indicates undercooking. Roasting times are given on pages11 and 23. For accompaniments see the following page.

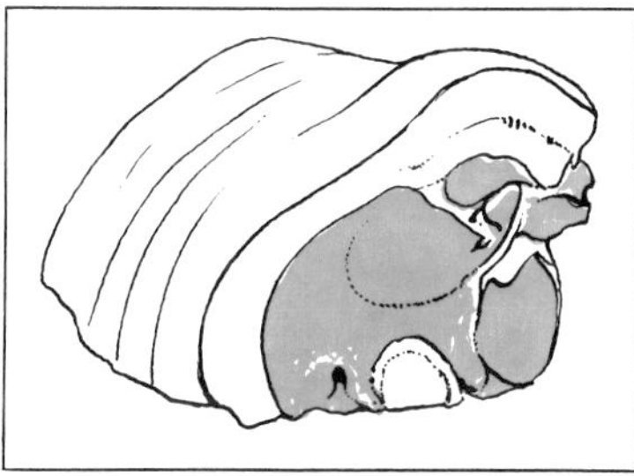

Loin

Loin is a joint that varies in size. It is cut from the top end down to the chump end. For easy carving, ask the butcher to chine the joint.

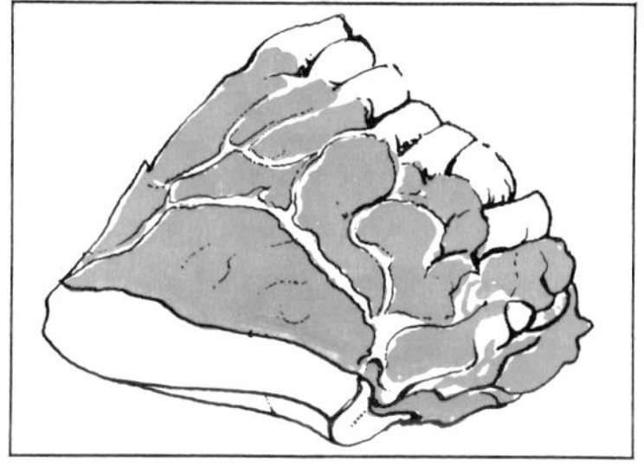

Spare rib

Good small joint for roasting or pot roasting.

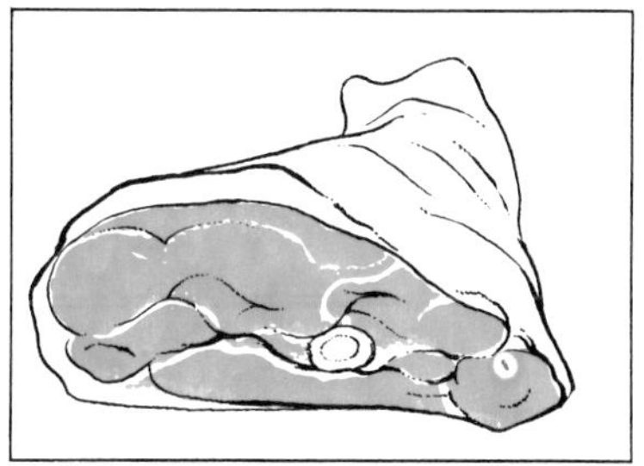

Leg

A large joint weighing 10 lb or more. This is usually sold halved, knuckle or fillet end, or boned, rolled and cut into smaller joints. Make sure that the skin is well scored to give crisp crackling. A half leg can be boned and stuffed.

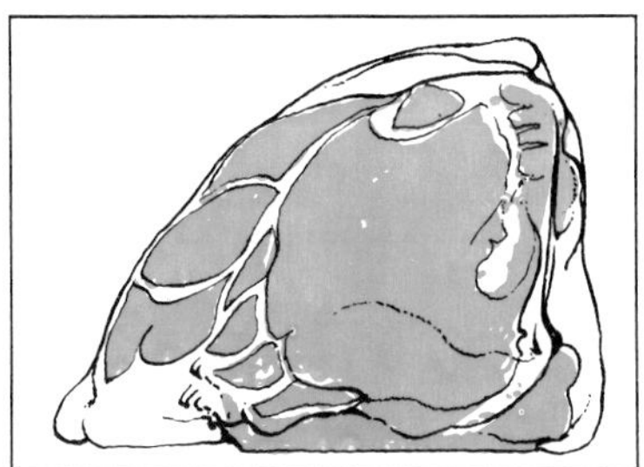

Blade bone or boned, rolled shoulder joints

Joints weighing 2-3$\frac{1}{2}$ lb, suitable for small family meals. The meat is sweet and tender but, since the joints are cut from the forequarter, do not expect the crackling to be crisp.

Accompaniments to pork roasts

Apple sauce

1 lb cooking apples
rind of ½ lemon
1 dessertspoon caster sugar
½ oz butter

Method

Peel and core the apples. Pare the lemon rind thinly. Put apples and rind in a saucepan with 2-3 tablespoons water. Cover tightly and cook until pulpy. Beat with a wooden spoon until smooth, or put through a strainer. Stir in the sugar and butter. Serve hot.

Sage and onion stuffing

3 medium-size onions
2 oz butter, or suet
6 oz fresh white breadcrumbs
2 teaspoons dried sage
1 teaspoon chopped parsley
salt and pepper
beaten egg, or milk

Method

Slice onions finely and boil 15-20 minutes in salted water. Drain and stir in the butter or suet. Add remaining ingredients, season well and mix with beaten egg or milk. If the joint is not suitable for stuffing, put the mixture into a small ovenproof dish, baste with 1 tablespoon of dripping and cook in the oven for 30-40 minutes at 400°F or Mark 6.

Braised cabbage

1 firm white cabbage
1 large onion
1 oz butter
1 cooking apple (peeled and sliced)
salt and pepper
1-2 tablespoons stock (see page 155)

Method

Cut the cabbage in quarters and cut away the core. Shred finely. If you are using hard white Dutch cabbage, blanch by putting into boiling, salted water for 1 minute, draining and refreshing with 1 cup of cold water. This is not necessary for green cabbage. Slice the onion and put in a flameproof casserole with the butter. Cook over gentle heat until soft but not coloured. Add the cabbage to the pan with the peeled and sliced apple. Season, stir well and pour in the stock. Cover with non-stick (silicone) cooking paper and lid, and cook for 45-50 minutes on the bottom shelf of the oven at 325°F or Mark 3.

Braised leeks

6 leeks
1 oz butter

Method

Set the oven at 325°F or Mark 3. Trim the leeks, make a cross cut in the top and wash thoroughly under running water. Blanch by putting into boiling, salted water for 1 minute. Drain well. Put in a well-buttered casserole, cover tightly and cook for 45-50 minutes on the bottom shelf of the pre-set oven.

Roast leg of pork with a sage and onion stuffing is good served with baked (roast) potatoes, braised leeks and apple sauce. The outside skin of the pork has been well scored to give crisp crackling

Roast pork périgourdine

4 lb loin, or $\frac{1}{2}$ leg, of pork
salt
pepper (ground from mill)
1 clove of garlic
$\frac{1}{4}$- $\frac{1}{2}$ pint water
$\frac{1}{2}$ pint demi-glace sauce (to serve — see page 153)

The region of **Périgord** in the southwest of France is famous for its good cooking and especially for its foie gras and large truffles.

Among the less extravagant dishes, according to the late gourmet and author M. Boulestin, is our recipe here for roast pork. The long slow roasting of a loin or leg of pork is characteristic of Périgord, where people used to have their meat cooked by the baker (after the bread had been baked) as the majority had no ovens of their own. Though this dish is traditionally served cold, here we serve it hot with a demi-glace sauce and accompanying vegetables.

Method

Set oven at 325 F or Mark 3. Remove the skin and bone from the loin or leg, flatten the meat and season very well with salt and pepper. Split the garlic into 5-6 thin shreds and place these along the meat. Roll the meat and tie securely, sprinkle again with salt and pepper and put into an ovenproof dish with $\frac{1}{4}$ pint water.

Note : if you want pork crackling, we suggest that when removing the skin from the raw meat you cut away $\frac{1}{4}$ inch of fat with it. Cut this skin in strips and cook in a separate tin in the oven for 50-60 minutes, or until golden-brown and crisp. Serve the crackling lightly salted as an accompaniment.

Cook the pork, allowing 40 minutes per lb, but not less than 2 hours for a smaller joint than given above. Baste it occasionally during the cooking, adding extra water when liquid reduces to a glaze. Meanwhile make the demi-glace sauce.

Take up the meat, remove the string and cut in thin slices, spoon over any juices left in the dish. Heat up the demi-glace sauce and hand separately.

Right : removing the skin and bone from the loin of pork before flattening it so that it can be rolled and tied easily. Below : the cooked pork

Loin of pork alsacienne

2-2$\frac{1}{2}$ lb loin of pork (chined)
$\frac{1}{2}$ pint stock (made with chine bone, 1 onion and 1 carrot, both sliced, and bouquet garni — see page 155)
salt and pepper
2-3 tablespoons dripping
fresh white breadcrumbs (optional)
1 tablespoon plain flour

For cabbage mixture
1 small Dutch cabbage
1 oz butter
1 onion (finely sliced)
1 lemon
salt and pepper
4 dessert apples
parsley (chopped) - to garnish
2 hard-boiled eggs (to garnish)

Method

If the pork has rind, score it well and rub with salt before roasting. Baste well with hot dripping and cook for 1$\frac{1}{4}$ hours in the oven, pre-set at 400°F or Mark 6. If the pork has no rind, cover the fat with fresh breadcrumbs, baste well and return to the oven to brown 20 minutes before end of cooking time.

Meanwhile prepare cabbage mixture : cut cabbage in four, remove the hard core and shred leaves finely. Blanch in boiling salted water for 1 minute, then drain, refresh in cold water and tip into a basin.

Melt the butter in a flameproof casserole, add the onion, cover and cook slowly until soft but not coloured. Turn into the basin of cabbage and mix well together. Peel and slice lemon, mix with the cabbage and season. Peel and quarter the apples and cut away the core. Arrange the quarters, rounded side down, at the bottom of the casserole. Spoon the cabbage mixture on top of the apple, cover with well-buttered paper and put on the casserole lid. Cook gently on top of the stove for 15-20 minutes, then put in the oven on a shelf under the pork and continue cooking for 30-40 minutes.

Take up the meat. Tip off the dripping from the roasting tin, keeping back any sediment, stir in 1 tablespoon flour and cook slowly until brown. Pour on $\frac{1}{2}$ pint stock, season and boil up well. Strain. Slice the meat, lay on a hot serving dish and pour the gravy over.

Run a palette knife round the side of the casserole and turn the cabbage on to a hot dish — it should fall out in a flat cake. Scatter the chopped parsley on the top and surround with quartered hard-boiled eggs.

Stewing

Stewing means cooking food gently in liquid. In general, meat used for stewing is not from the most expensive cuts, but from those that require long, slow cooking to make them tender

and to bring out their flavour. Cuts with a slight marbling of fat or gristle are excellent stewed, and this marbling makes meat more succulent.

A stew can be either white or brown. In a white stew, sometimes called a fricassée, the meat is not browned but blanched to whiten and to take away strong flavours before cooking. The liquid is usually thickened after the meat has been cooked, or towards the end, as in Irish stew, when the potatoes break up to thicken the gravy. A white stew is usually cooked on top of the stove.

In a brown stew, sometimes called a ragoût, meat is browned with or without vegetables and a little flour is stirred in just before the stock is added. It may be cooked either on top of the stove, or inside the oven.

Liquid in both brown and white stews must never be allowed to do more than simmer, since boiling will only toughen meat.

A stew may be an everyday dish, but it is easily turned into a party special by adding wine, cream or a garnish.

Preparation of stews

White stew. Soak meat well, preferably overnight, in plenty of cold salted water. Change the water once or twice during this process to take away any strong flavour. Then rinse and put into the pan ready for cooking; cover with fresh cold water, add salt and — for veal or rabbit — a slice of lemon to whiten meat. Blanch by bringing slowly to the boil, then skim, drain and refresh in cold water to wash away any scum. Return to the pan and add liquid specified in the recipe, usually just enough to cover meat.

Veal or chicken stock, not water, should be used, because it will make a much better sauce. Chicken does not need soaking unless it is jointed raw, and a boiling fowl should be blanched. Keep the pan covered.

Brown stew. The pan is very important in the making of a brown stew. Choose a thick, enamelled iron pan or flame-proof casserole, so that the stew can be cooked and served in it. Failing this, brown the meat in a frying pan and transfer it to a casserole, but make the sauce or gravy in the same frying pan to avoid losing any flavour.

Cut meat (without bone) into 2-inch squares, leaving on a small amount of fat. Gristle appears only in shin or chuck steak and any white streaks may be left on. Cuts with bone should be divided into slightly larger pieces.

Heat pan or casserole well before putting in the dripping or oil. Put in meat just to cover bottom of pan, and leave enough room to turn pieces comfortably. Fry on full heat for beef (not so fierce for veal or lamb) until meat is evenly browned (about $3\frac{1}{2}$ minutes). Turn each piece and brown for the same time on the other side. Do not fry for longer than 7 minutes.

Now take out meat, keep hot and add vegetables as specified in recipe. Lower heat and allow to colour. Pour off all excess fat but for 1-2 tablespoons. Add flour (about 1 dessertspoon — 1 tablespoon for $\frac{3}{4}$-1 pint stock); use slightly less if stock is jellied. Colour flour slowly for 2-3 minutes, scraping it gently from bottom of pan or casserole with a metal spoon.

Now add stock (1 pint for $1\frac{1}{2}$ lb solid meat). It is better to add two-thirds of the given quantity first, and bring it to the boil. Replace meat. Then add remainder of stock so that it comes just below level of meat. Add specified flavouring, cover pan or casserole tightly and cook as specified in the recipe.

If pre-cooking a stew ready for eating later on, transfer to a cold container so that it cools quickly; when reheating, bring to the boil before keeping warm (the high temperature will kill any bacteria that may be present).

The following cuts are the best for stewing:

Beef : chuck or shoulder steak (cut from the blade bone); clod; sticking; skirt.

Mutton or lamb : middle neck; double scrag or scrag; fillet end of leg.

Veal : breast; knuckle; cuts from the shoulder.

Rabbit : wild rabbit or tame (Ostend) rabbit in joints or whole.

When a cut contains a fair quantity of bone, as with neck or breast, allow a little more than for cuts that are solid meat.

Types of stew

Fricassée. This describes various stews of meat, poultry, fish or vegetables, usually made with a white stock. In France this term refers almost exclusively to a poultry dish in a white sauce.

Ragoût (brown). Pieces of meat, poultry or fish are lightly browned and then slowly cooked in stock to which vegetables are added.

Salmis. This is a type of ragoût, usually of game or poultry. The meat is first lightly roasted, then jointed and gently simmered for a short time in a rich, brown sauce.

Blanquette. This is a white ragoût of lamb, veal, chicken or rabbit, bound with egg yolks and cream, and sometimes garnished with small onions and mushrooms.

Navarin. This is the French word for a mutton or lamb stew made with root vegetables.

Certain vegetables are good stewed on their own, especially white ones such as onions, celery, artichokes and chicory.

Irish stew

2-2 ½ lb scrag, or middle neck of mutton, or lamb
¾ lb onions
1 ½ lb potatoes
1 ½ pints water
1 tablespoon mushroom ketchup (optional)
salt and pepper

The meat can be a mixture of scrag and middle neck ; in the days of large households a forequarter of lamb was used. To help tenderise meat and take out some of its red colour, soak it in a little salty water over night or 2-3 hours before using.

Method

Set oven at 325°F or Mark 3.

Trim meat after soaking, draining and drying it. Cut into pieces. Slice or quarter onions ; wash and slice potatoes thickly, or cut into chunks.

Layer meat and vegetables together in a casserole, starting and finishing with potatoes, and season well. Mix water and ketchup together and pour over. Cover tightly and cook in the pre-set oven for at least 2 hours.

Avoid stirring but take the casserole out and shake it occasionally to ensure that the stew is not sticking. Dish up when meat is very tender and gravy thick and rich. Like most stews, it reheats well, but it must be brought to boiling point before keeping hot.

Watchpoint Long, slow cooking is essential so that the gravy is thickened and enriched by the potato and onion which will cook down to a purée.

Navarin of lamb

2 lb middle neck of lamb, or mutton
2 carrots
1 small piece of swede, or turnip
2 onions
1 rounded tablespoon dripping
pinch of granulated sugar (optional)
1 rounded dessertspoon plain flour
¾ pint stock (see page 155). or water
salt and pepper
bouquet garni

Method

Cut and trim the cutlets, taking out any superfluous bone. Cut the carrots and swede or turnip into short thick strips ; quarter the onions.

Heat a shallow, flameproof casserole or pan, put in the dripping and, when hot, lay in the meat. Brown cutlets on both sides (do this in two lots, if necessary). Then take out the meat, put in the vegetables and fry more slowly until they are just coloured. A good pinch of sugar may be added to help this colouring process.

Now stir in the flour and, 1 minute later, add the stock or water. Bring to boiling point, replace meat in casserole or pan and make sure that the liquid comes just level with the meat. Season, add the bouquet garni, cover the pan and simmer gently for about 1 hour or until the meat is tender. Turn the cutlets from time to time. Serve with creamed potatoes.

Ragoût of beef with celery and walnuts

$1\frac{1}{2}$ lb chuck steak, or skirt
12 button onions
2 tablespoons dripping, or bacon fat
1 rounded dessertspoon plain flour
1 wineglass red wine
bouquet garni
1 clove of garlic (crushed with salt)
1 pint stock (see page 155)
salt and pepper
1 head of celery
$\frac{1}{2}$ oz butter
1 oz walnuts (shelled)
1 dessertspoon shredded orange rind

Method

Cut beef into 2-inch squares and peel onions. Heat thick casserole and put in fat. When hot, lay in pieces of meat; fry until brown, turning pieces once. Take out meat, add onions and fry slowly until beginning to colour. Draw off heat, drain so that only 1 tablespoon of fat is left in the casserole. Stir in flour, add red wine, meat, bouquet garni and garlic. Barely cover with stock, season, bring slowly to the boil, cover and

simmer gently until tender ($1\frac{1}{2}$-2 hours).

Meanwhile, cut the trimmed head of celery into slices crossways. Heat the butter in a frying pan, put in walnuts and celery and toss over the heat with a pinch of salt, keeping celery crisp. Then shred and cook orange rind in boiling water until tender, drain and rinse. Dish up ragoût, or leave in casserole for serving, and scatter celery mixture on the top with the orange rind.

Left : slices of celery and walnuts are tossed in butter over the heat. This garnish goes well with finished ragoût of beef (below)

Ragoût of lamb with savoury rice

½ leg of lamb, shank, or fillet end (about 2 lb)
1½ oz butter
2 onions (thinly sliced)
1 clove of garlic (crushed)
1 tablespoon paprika pepper
1 tablespoon plain flour
1 teaspoon tomato purée
1 wineglass white wine, or 1 wineglass dry vermouth (optional)
½ pint stock (made with the bone from the meat — see page 155)
salt and pepper
bouquet garni, or pinch of mixed dried herbs

For savoury rice
5 oz long grain rice
salt
3 streaky bacon rashers
4 oz mushrooms
1 small packet frozen peas, or 1 cup of cooked peas
4 medium-size tomatoes
1 oz butter

Method

Bone out the meat well before cooking time (or ask butcher to do it) so that a good stock can be made from the bone. Cut meat into 2-inch squares, leaving on a little fat. Heat pan or flameproof casserole. Drop in butter and, when foaming, put in the meat. Fry briskly until meat is just brown, turning occasionally. Keep heat slightly lower for lamb than for beef.

Take out meat and keep hot. Put in onions and garlic. Cook for 4-5 minutes, stirring occasionally, then add paprika and flour. Stir in tomato purée, wine and stock. Bring to boil, season, tip out into bowl and replace meat in pan. Now pour over sauce. Add bouquet garni (or dried herbs), cover tightly and cook gently for about 1 hour, or until meat is tender, on top of the stove, or inside the oven at 350°F or Mark 3.

To make savoury rice : boil it in plenty of salted water until tender (10-12 minutes). Strain into a colander, rinse with hot water and make drainage holes with a spoon handle ; leave for 30 minutes. Meanwhile, cut rind and rust from bacon, then cut rashers in short, thick strips. Slice mushrooms and cook peas. Scald, peel and quarter tomatoes ; flick out seeds and then cut away the hard stalk : halve the quarters lengthways.

Heat a large frying pan, drop in the butter and, when foaming, put in bacon and mushrooms. Fry gently for 4-5 minutes, then add rice, peas and tomatoes. Season well. Fork up over brisk heat for 2 minutes until thoroughly hot. Then turn into a serving dish.

Dish up lamb after removing the bouquet garni.

Note : if white wine is not available, dry vermouth is a good substitute. If you have neither, use just under ¼ pint extra stock.

Fricassée of rabbit

4-5 pieces of Ostend rabbit, or 1 wild rabbit (jointed)
white stock (see page 156), or water (to cover meat)
2 onions (sliced)
bouquet garni
2 oz button mushrooms
½ oz butter

For sauce
1½ oz butter
3 tablespoons plain flour
¼ pint creamy milk

Method

Soak rabbit thoroughly in salted water, changing it from time to time. Blanch by putting into cold water, bringing to the boil, draining and refreshing. Trim away any pieces of skin with scissors and neaten the joints. Put rabbit into a shallow pan, barely cover with stock or water and add sliced onions.

For a more delicate flavour, blanch the onions first (by putting into cold water and bringing to the boil). Put in the bouquet garni, cover and simmer for 1-2 hours, or until very tender. Ostend rabbit takes less time than wild rabbit. Then drain off liquid, which should measure about ¾ pint.

Now make a roux in a saucepan with the butter and flour (see page 157), cook for about ½ minute, cool a little and strain on the liquid. Blend and stir until boiling. Boil gently until it is the consistency of thick cream ; add the milk and continue cooking. At the same time, sauté the mushrooms in butter in another pan. Add these to the sauce and pour it over the rabbit. Turn the fricassée into a covered dish and leave in a warm oven for 5 minutes before serving. This allows the flavour of the sauce to penetrate the meat.

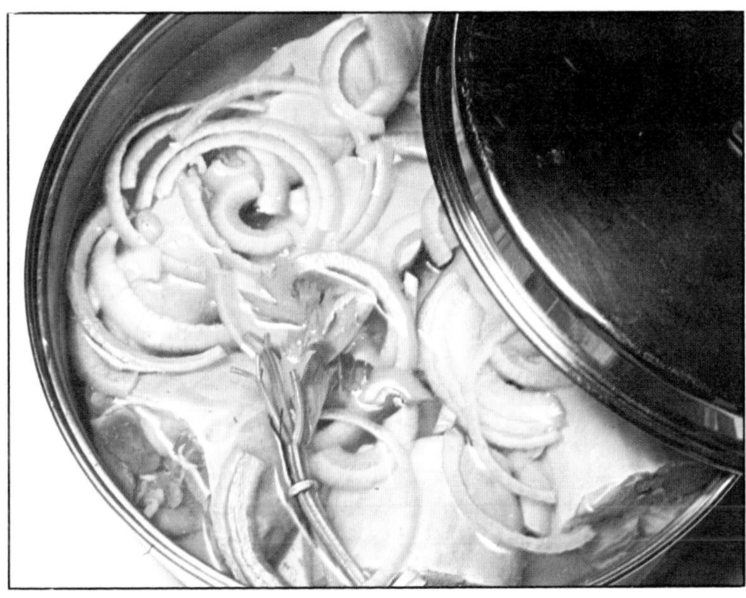

Blanquette of veal

$2\frac{1}{4}$ lb breast of veal
2 medium-size carrots (quartered)
2 medium-size onions (quartered)
bouquet garni
pinch of salt
$1\frac{1}{2}$ pints stock (see page 156), or water

For sauce
$1\frac{1}{2}$ oz butter
3 tablespoons plain flour
1-2 egg yolks
$\frac{1}{4}$ pint creamy milk
squeeze of lemon juice

Traditionally, breast of veal is used for this dish to get a rich, jellied stock from bones. But a greater proportion of shoulder meat can be added, ie. twice as much as breast. Breast of lamb can replace the veal.

Method

Cut meat into chunks (ask your butcher to do this if you are using breast of lamb and also trim off excess fat — otherwise cook in the same way). Soak overnight in cold water, blanch, drain and refresh.

Put the meat into a large pan with the quartered carrots and onions. Add bouquet garni, salt and barely cover with the stock or water. Cover and simmer for 1-$1\frac{1}{4}$ hours until very tender and a bone can be pulled from a piece of meat.

Draw pan aside and pour off all liquid, cover pan and keep hot. The stock should measure 1 pint. If it is more, turn into a pan and boil to reduce to 1 pint.

To prepare the sauce : melt the butter in a separate pan, stir in the flour, cook for 1-2 seconds without letting the butter brown, draw aside and allow to cool slightly. Pour on the stock, blend, then stir until boiling. Boil briskly for 3-4 minutes until sauce is creamy in consistency and then draw aside.

Mix yolks with milk in a bowl, add a little of the hot sauce, then pour mixture slowly back into the bulk of the sauce. Taste for seasoning and add the lemon juice. Pour sauce over veal, shake pan gently to mix all together. Cover and keep hot for 15 minutes before serving so that the flavour of the sauce can penetrate the meat. Turn meat and vegetables into a clean hot dish and serve with creamed potatoes or boiled rice.

For a party dish, single cream instead of milk can be used for the sauce, but if you decide to do this, take out the onions and carrots before serving and replace them with a mixture of previously cooked peas, baby carrots and button onions.

Ragoût of beef bourguignon

$1\frac{1}{2}$ lb chuck steak
2 3 tablespoons oil, or dripping
3 oz green streaky bacon rasher
$\frac{1}{4}$ lb button onions (peeled)
1 tablespoon plain flour
1 clove of garlic (crushed)
1 teaspoon tomato purée
bouquet garni
2 wineglasses red Burgundy, or Burgundy-type wine
$\frac{1}{4}$-$\frac{1}{2}$ pint stock (see page 155)
salt and pepper
4-6 oz button mushrooms
parsley (chopped)
croûtes (small triangles of fried bread)

A beef ragoût cooked with red wine is correctly known as beef à la bourguignonne, although many French restaurants call it boeuf bourguignon. The traditional garnish consists of lean bacon, glazed onions and mushrooms.

Method

Cut meat into 2-inch squares. Heat fat in a pan or flameproof casserole, put in meat and brown quickly but thoroughly on all sides. Take out meat and keep hot.

Cut bacon into thick strips and blanch with the onions by putting them into cold water and bringing to the boil for 2 minutes. Drain, add both bacon and onions to pan and brown slowly. Remove onions, draw pan aside, stir in flour, cook for 1 minute, then add garlic, tomato purée, meat and bouquet garni.

Watchpoint It is advisable to remove onions from casserole after browning, replacing them in the ragoût after the first hour, otherwise they tend to become mushy and spoil the appearance of the dish.

Boil wine to reduce a little and add to pan with half of the stock.

Bring slowly to the boil, shaking pan gently and adding more stock just to cover the meat. Season lightly, cover tightly and simmer until tender ($1\frac{1}{2}$-2 hours), replacing onions after 1 hour.

About 15 minutes before end of cooking time, add mushrooms, whole. Fry croûtes in a little oil and butter until crisp. Dish up ragoût, dust with chopped parsley and garnish with croûtes.

Ragoût of beef bourguignon garnished with croûtes of bread and onions

Cassoulet

1 lb haricot beans (soaked and pre-cooked — see right)
6 oz salt belly pork, or green streaky bacon
4 cloves of garlic (finely chopped)
½ shoulder of mutton, or half a duck
2 tablespoons good beef dripping, or bacon fat, or butter
bouquet garni
salt and black pepper
4 oz garlic, or pork, sausage
¾ lb ripe tomatoes, or 1 medium size (12 oz) can
1 dessertspoon tomato purée
1 teaspoon granulated sugar
browned breadcrumbs

This is a traditional dish from the Languedoc region of France and it contains many specialities of that region. The following recipe is simplified, with mutton replacing the traditional pickled goose. If preferred, half a duck could be used. Garlic sausage can be obtained at most delicatessens, or you can use a pork sausage.

Method

Drain the beans and put into a large fireproof casserole with the pork or bacon and the finely chopped garlic. Pour in water to cover well, put on lid, simmer gently for 1-1¼ hours. Drain, set aside and reserve liquor.

Bone the mutton and cut into large cubes or leave the duck in one piece. Fry until golden brown in the dripping, add the beans and pork to the casserole with the herbs, a little salt and a lot of black pepper. Moisten with some of the bean liquor, cover and stew very slowly for 3-4 hours, adding a little more of the cooking liquor from time to time, if necessary. After 2½ hours' cooking, add the sausage. When the beans are tender, take out pork, remove skin and slice; also slice the sausage; replace pork (or bacon) and sausage in casserole.

Cook the tomatoes to a pulp in a separate pan, add the tomato purée and season with salt, pepper and sugar. Spoon this mixture over the beans, shake the casserole gently to mix it in, then sprinkle the top of the beans with the browned crumbs. Put in hot oven, pre-set at 375°F or Mark 5, for a further ¾-1 hour to brown.

Dried haricot beans

1 Wash the beans and pick them over to remove any grit or small stones.
2 Soak them in plenty of tepid water for 8 hours, or leave overnight. If they have to be left longer, change the water or they may start to ferment.
3 Drain them, cover with plenty of fresh warm water and cook in a covered pan. If the water is hard, add a pinch of bicarbonate of soda which will help to soften the outer skins. Salt is never added at this stage as it would harden them. Bring beans very slowly to boiling point, allowing 30-40 minutes, then simmer gently for about 1 hour. Drain them again and then use as specified in the recipe.

Grilling and accompaniments

As a method of cooking, grilling has certain advantages ; it is quick, straightforward and good for a meal which has to be on the table in a hurry ; it is ideal for the diet-conscious because grills have little fat and almost no liquid. However, cuts have to be of the best quality, so a grill is not a cheap dish. On the following pages, you will find basic rules for grilling, together with recipes for grills, savoury butters and sauces.

Since a grill is a last-minute dish and one that should be served at once, it is not easy for the cook/hostess. Some grills such as cutlets, chops and kebabs can be kept hot for a short time in the grill pan with the juices, and heat turned low. Steaks, however, should be served at once. All grilling calls for a certain amount of attention, especially gammon steaks which tend to be dry unless brushed with melted butter or oil every 2-3 minutes.

The grill should be turned on at least 5-6 minutes before use to get the maximum heat. While it is heating leave grill pan underneath with grid set at right height. If food is getting overcooked when actually grilling, lower grid rather than grill heat.

Do not salt meat before grilling ; this causes juices to run, making food less succulent, but it may be peppered (ground from mill). Then brush meat with oil, turn over once or twice while grilling, keeping well brushed with oil (or as specified in individual recipe).

Buy the best cooking oil you can afford. Olive oil is the finest, but you can also use groundnut, or corn-based, oil instead. It is more economical to buy large tins or bottles. The given times for grilling are approximate, depending on the grill, thickness of food and whether or not it is to be pink inside or well done. A rule-of-thumb guide for steak is to press with your fingers : if it gives like a sponge, it is rare ; if firmer and more resilient — medium rare ; or firm with no resilience — well done.

How to 'dry' fry

If your grill is not a very efficient one or you have a solid fuel cooker, use the method known as dry frying. Take a thick, heavy frying pan — iron, ridged or enamelled iron, or cast aluminium. Set on full heat for several minutes, then put in 1 tablespoon of oil or dripping (free from gravy) and when hot put in meat. Keep on full heat until well browned on one side, pressing the food well down with a palette knife ; then turn and brown on the other side.

Time this process and lower heat if necessary to complete cooking. The time will vary, depending on what is being grilled and how well cooked it is to be (see chart on pages 54-55).

Grills should be accompanied by savoury butters (see page 66) served separately or in pats on top of steak, cutlets, etc. Grilled meats look best when served plainly garnished with a sprig of watercress and chip / jacket potatoes. A mixed green salad also goes well with a grill. For accompanying vegetables, see pages 61-64.

Mixed grill

STEAK CUTS

Rump ($1\frac{1}{2}$ lb slice, 1 inch thick, serves 3-4)
This steak has incomparable flavour but to be tender must be well hung. A guide to this is the colour, which should have a purplish tinge with creamy-white fat. It improves if brushed with oil 1-2 hours before grilling. During grilling time brush once or twice with oil to prevent scorching.

Sirloin or entrecôte ($\frac{3}{4}$-1 inch thick, serves 1)
This steak is cut from the top part of the sirloin.

Minute ($\frac{1}{2}$ inch thick, serves 1)
Thin slice of entrecôte. This steak should be cooked very rapidly and to get it properly browned without over-cooking, dry fry rather than grill.

T-Bone ($1\frac{1}{2}$-2 inches thick, serves 2-3)
A whole slice cut from the sirloin with the bone.

Porterhouse ($1\frac{1}{2}$-2 inches thick, serves 1-2)
A slice cut from the wing rib, taken off the bone.

Fillet (1-$1\frac{1}{2}$ inches thick, serves 1)
The most expensive and possibly most tender of steaks. There is a large demand for these slices cut across the fillet, so they are in short supply. The fillet (averaging 6-7 lb) lies under the sirloin and there is a comparatively small proportion of fillet in relation to the weight of the rest of the animal. Dry fry or grill.

Tournedos (1-$1\frac{1}{2}$ inches thick, serves 1)
These are cut from the 'eye' of the fillet, ie. from centre after it has been trimmed (fillet steaks include the side or edges, ie. trimmings). A tournedos is very much a delicacy and may be served plainly grilled or dry fried with a garnish as for a fillet steak, or as a dish such as tournedos chasseur. The crisp dry fat in which fillet is encased (kidney suet) is very special; a small nut of this may be fried or grilled to top each tournedos.

Chateaubriand (3-4 inches thick, serves 2)
A thick cut taken from the heart of the fillet. This steak, once grilled or dry fried, is sliced downwards for serving.

GRILLING TIMES		ACCOMPANIMENTS
Rare : Medium rare : Well done :	6-7 minutes 8-10 minutes 14-16 minutes	Maître d'hôtel or garlic butter, chip or jacket potatoes and fried onions. Vegetables : runner or French beans ; peas ; green salad.
Rare : Medium rare : Well done ;	5 minutes 6-7 minutes 9-10 minutes	Maître d'hôtel or garlic butter, chip or jacket potatoes. Vegetables : chicory with butter ; peperoni ; green salad. (See recipe for sirloin steak provençale, page 60)
Rare : Medium rare :	1-1 $\frac{1}{2}$ minutes 2-3 minutes	Maître d'hôtel or garlic butter, garnish with watercress ; chip potatoes and green salad.
Rare : Medium rare :	7-8 minutes 8-10 minutes	Maître d'hôtel or garlic butter, chip or jacket potatoes.
Rare : Medium rare :	7-8 minutes 8-10 minutes	Maître d'hôtel or garlic butter, chip or jacket potatoes.
Rare : Medium rare to well done :	6 minutes 7-8 minutes	Béarnaise sauce or juices from the pan. Garnish with mushrooms, or peperoni, chip potatoes. (See recipe for peppered steak page 59).
Rare : Medium rare to well done :	6 minutes 7-8 minutes	Béarnaise sauce, or other sauces and vegetables according to recipe.
Rare to medium rare :	16-20 minutes	Béarnaise sauce (see page 152), and château potatoes. For savoury butters, see page 66.

Lamb

Cutlets

These are taken from the best end of neck and though cutlets may be bought ready-cut and trimmed, it is more economical to buy the neck and prepare them at home.

Ask the butcher to chine the neck for you, that is to saw the half backbone (chine bone) through so that the cutlets can be easily divided. He will also saw through the end bones to shorten them by about 2-3 inches. Cut away this 'flap' which can then be divided into 4-5 pieces and grilled with the cutlets. The chine bone is also detached and used for broth or gravy. A whole best end contains 6-7 cutlet bones with an average weight of $1\frac{1}{2}$-2 lb, depending on the size of the animal.

Cutlets must be plump, otherwise they curl when grilled or dry fried and become dry and tasteless. If the neck is medium size, allow 5 cutlets from a whole piece of best end ; this gives a nut of meat $\frac{3}{4}$-1 inch thick.

Divide the neck into cutlets with a sharp knife, taking two bones if necessary. Cut out the second bone and any excess fat. Leave a rim of fat (about $\frac{1}{4}$ inch) round the meat and the small piece that lies just under it. Scrape the bone clean.

To be attractive, cutlets must be well trimmed ; fat trimmings can be rendered down for use as dripping.

Brush with fat or oil and cook on grid or base of grilling pan for 7-8 minutes, turning once or twice and keeping well brushed with fat. The cutlets should be well browned with the fat crisp on the outside, and delicately pink when cut. Serve plain or with pats of savoury butter and sauté cucumber with spring onions or peas and baby carrots.

Noisettes

These are cutlets without the bone. Butchers will cut them for you, but you can prepare them at home. Take the best end unchined and start boning at the chine bone end. Use a small sharp knife and with short strokes cut down to, and along, the cutlet bones. Keep the knife well pressed on to the bones to avoid cutting into meat.

When the bone is out, season cut surface of the meat and roll up, starting at chine end. Trim off the end piece if there is more than enough to wrap once round the nut of meat. Tie securely at 1-$1\frac{1}{4}$ inch intervals with fine string, then cut between each tie. Grill as for lamb cutlets.

Chops

Loin chops are bought ready-cut and trimmed, and are 1-$1\frac{1}{2}$ inches thick.

Brush with oil and grill 8-9 minutes as for lamb cutlets. They should be well browned but slightly pink when cut. Serve with savoury butter. Best vegetables are runner beans ; courgettes in butter ; new or creamed potatoes.

Kebabs

The traditional shashlik, ie. skewer, dish consists of square chunks of meat, usually lamb, cut from the shoulder or leg and threaded on to long metal skewers, interspersed with slices of onion and bayleaves. But a mixture can be made from chipolata sausages, bacon rolls and pieces of lamb or fillet steak. Put these on a skewer, brush with melted butter and grill, turning skewer to cook chunks evenly. Dish up on boiled rice.

Kidneys

Lamb's kidneys are a classic ingredient of a mixed grill. To prepare, carefully peel off the hard fat which encases them (imported kidneys have this already removed). This suet rendered down, makes an excellent frying fat or dripping.

Skin kidneys by nicking the skin on the rounded side and drawing it back towards the core. Pull gently to get out as much of the core as possible before cutting away the skin. Split open on the rounded side and thread a skewer through to keep flat. Brush with melted butter, grill rounded side first and brush with melted butter from time to time throughout cooking. Allow 6-8 minutes grilling time according to size. Don't overcook or they become very leathery.

Serve kidneys with maître d'hôtel or anchovy butter.

Mixed grill

For a mixed grill, the following ingredients for one person are a guide: 1 cutlet, 1 kidney, 1 sausage, 1 tomato, 2 mushrooms, 1 rasher of bacon, watercress and maître d'hôtel butter.

First prepare cutlets and kidneys as directed. Do not prick sausages as this makes them more likely to burst when cooking. Halve tomatoes and season cut surface. Peel the mushrooms (preferably large, flat ones) and cut stalks level with caps. De-rind and flatten bacon.

Grill tomatoes, rounded side first, and turn after 3-4 minutes. Dust tops with caster sugar, put a knob of butter on each and grill for the same time. Grill mushrooms in the same way, putting a knob of butter on each side. Lift on to a plate and keep hot. Grill bacon, then the sausages, allowing 7-8 minutes, turning them once. Dish up with tomatoes and mushrooms. Keep hot. Grill the cutlets and add to the dish. Top with kidneys and maître d'hôtel butter, garnish dish with watercress.

Pork

Chops

Loin chops are really the only cut of pork suitable for grilling. Trim neatly, remove surplus fat and brush with melted butter. Heat grill well and cook chops thoroughly for 5-7 minutes on each side, brushing with butter.

Garnish with watercress and serve with an apple or barbecue sauce, sauté or chip potatoes and salad.

Gammon steaks

These are $\frac{1}{2}$-inch slices from the gammon of bacon which may be smoked or green, ie. unsmoked. The latter is milder in flavour. Cut away the rind and brush well with melted butter while grilling. Set the grid lower in the grill pan than for other meats. Allow about 7-8 minutes grilling time.

Garnish with fried pineapple slices. Serve with spinach, or runner or French beans, or peas and chip or sauté potatoes.

Garrick steak

1 ½ lb rump steak (piece cut about 1½ inches thick)
brushing of salad oil

For mushroom filling
1 shallot, or 1 teaspoon onion (finely chopped)
½ oz butter
4 oz mushrooms
1 teaspoon each chopped parsley and thyme
1 rounded tablespoon chopped ham
1 tablespoon fresh white bread-crumbs
salt and pepper
parsley butter (for serving) — see page 66

Trussing needle and fine string, or poultry pins lacers

This recipe serves 3-4.

Method

First prepare filling : soften the chopped shallot or onion in the butter. Wash mushrooms, chop finely and add to the pan with the herbs. Cover and cook 5-7 minutes. Draw aside and add ham, crumbs and seasoning. Turn out and cool.

Slit the steak on one side to form a pocket, fill with the purée and sew up with a trussing needle and fine string, or secure with poultry pins / lacers. Brush steak with a little salad oil and grill 4-5 minutes on each side.

Before serving remove string or pins / lacers. Slice downwards in ¼-inch slices and serve with parsley butter.

Rump steak filled and sewn with fine string, ready to be grilled

Minute steak soubise

5-6 minute steaks
1 oz butter (for frying)
1 lb onions (thinly sliced)

For sauce
1-2 oz butter
2 wineglasses red wine
salt
black pepper (ground from mill)
$\frac{1}{4}$ pint single cream
1 teaspoon arrowroot
2-3 tablespoons jellied stock (see page 155)l or bouillon cube mixed with water

Minute steaks are often chosen to be served plainly grilled, but this recipe has a delicious sauce for use on special occasions.

Method

Slice onions very thinly, fry slowly in 1 oz of butter until golden-brown. Add 1 glass of wine, season and cook slowly for 5-10 minutes. Strain onions (reserving the liquid) and place down centre of a serving dish.

Fry steaks quickly in butter, dish up on bed of onion.

To prepare sauce: tip the second glass of wine into the frying pan, boil up well and then add reserved liquid. Season and add the cream. Mix the arrowroot with the stock, add to the sauce and boil well. Spoon a little of this sauce over the meat and serve the rest separately.

Soubise denotes a purée of onions, usually mixed with rice, seasonings, butter and cream, or with a béchamel sauce instead of the rice.

Peppered steak

4 steaks (sirloin, minute or fillet)
black pepper (ground from mill)
oil (for frying)
watercress (to garnish)

For noisette butter
1-2 oz butter
juice of $\frac{1}{2}$ lemon

This dish, known as steak au poivre, is ideal for cooking at the table in a chafing dish or an electric frying pan, and is a good choice when you want to serve a straightforward yet fairly piquant dish.

Method

Grind black pepper liberally over the raw meat before sprinkling with oil and leave for 1-2 hours. Grill or dry fry, and time according to the cut (see page 54). Dish up, pour over noisette butter, garnish with watercress and serve at once with sauté potatoes and a green salad.

To prepare noisette butter: add the butter to the pan, allow it to brown, then at once add the lemon juice and pour, while still foaming, over the steaks.

Sirloin steak provençale

4 sirloin steaks
fat, or oil (for frying)

For salpicon

1 large onion
1 green and 2 red peppers
2 medium-size aubergines
salt
oil (for frying)
12 small black olives (stoned)

For sauce

2 shallots (chopped)
1 dessertspoon tomato purée
1 wineglass white wine
½ wineglass stock (see page 155)

Method

First prepare salpicon: slice onion into rounds, shred peppers and blanch by putting into boiling water and boiling for ½ minute before draining. Slice aubergines and sprinkle with salt. Fry onion in oil until golden-brown, add peppers and shake over the heat for a few minutes. Turn out and keep warm. Fry aubergines until brown and tender, add olives. Keep hot with onions and peppers.

Dry fry the steaks over high heat in fat or oil barely covering the base of a thick frying pan. Cook according to taste (see page 54). Dish up and cover each steak with the salpicon.

To make sauce: add shallots, tomato purée, wine and stock to same pan and boil up. Spoon sauce over the steaks and salpicon.

Provençale dishes make use of some of the vegetables characteristic of that region in southern France, such as tomatoes, peppers, aubergines, olives, and usually garlic.

Salpicon is the name given to a mixture of shredded ingredients usually bound with a rich sauce. This may be used as a garnish, a stuffing for pastry cases and other dishes, or be made into croquettes.

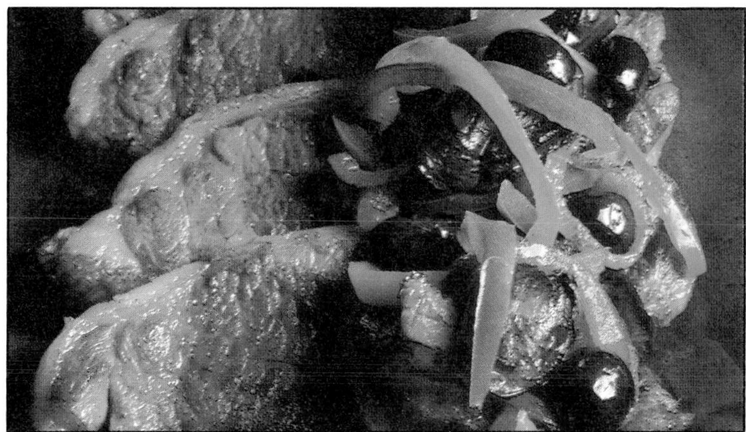

Vegetables to serve with grills

Stuffed mushrooms

2 mushrooms per person, and 2-3 over
$\frac{1}{2}$ oz butter
1 teaspoon chopped onion
1 tablespoon fresh white breadcrumbs, or slice of crust soaked in milk
salt and pepper
1 teaspoon chopped parsley
pinch of dried mixed herbs

Method

Cup mushrooms are best for this dish. Wash and peel them, then cut across the stalks level with the caps. Chop the trimmings with the extra mushrooms. Cook for 1-2 minutes in the butter with the chopped onion. Add the crumbs (or soaked crust, squeezed and broken up with a fork). Season and add herbs.

Spread this mixture on to the mushrooms, dot with butter and set them on a baking sheet, or in an ovenproof dish. Bake for 12-15 minutes in oven pre-set at 400°F or Mark 7, and serve in an ovenproof dish.

Fried onions

1 medium-size onion per person
2-3 tablespoons dripping, or oil
granulated sugar (for dusting)

Method

Peel onion, slice a small piece off the side so that the onion remains firmly on the chopping board while slicing fairly finely across (not lengthways). Push slices out into rings.

To make onions more digestible, blanch after slicing by putting into cold water and bringing to the boil. Refresh by pouring cold water over and draining well on absorbent paper.

Put slices into the frying pan with smoking hot fat or oil and fry fairly quickly, turning occasionally with a fork, dust with sugar to help them brown. When well browned take out and drain on absorbent paper before serving in heaps around, or on top of, steaks.

To peel onions

First cut off top and root with a sharp knife, then peel off first and second skins, or more (until onion is all white). Do not break the thin underskin — the oil released from here will make you cry.

To skin button onions easily, first scald (plunge into boiling water) for 1-2 minutes, then plunge into cold water.

Vegetables to serve with grills continued

Buttered courgettes

7-8 courgettes (according to size)
1-1½ oz butter
1 tablespoon water
salt and pepper
½ tablespoon chopped parsley
½ tablespoon fresh chopped mixed herbs — optional

Method

Wipe courgettes and trim stalks ; blanch them if large and firm, otherwise put direct into a pan or a flameproof casserole with butter and 1 tablespoon of water.

Add seasoning and press buttered paper on top ; cover with a lid (to conserve all juices). Cook slowly on top of stove for 15-20 minutes, or until tender. Garnish with chopped herbs.

Peperoni

2 green and 2 red peppers (halved, cored, seeds removed and thinly sliced)
1 oz butter
1 medium-size onion (sliced)
1 clove of garlic (crushed with ½ teaspoon salt)

Method

Prepare the peppers and blanch if wished. Melt the butter in a small pan, add the onion and crushed garlic and cook slowly until soft but not coloured, add the peppers and seasoning and cook until just tender.

Sauté cucumber

1 large cucumber
½-1 oz butter
1 bunch spring onions (trimmed), or 1 small onion (chopped)
salt and pepper
fresh mint (chopped) — to garnish

Method

Peel cucumber using a stainless steel knife ; split in four lengthways. Cut across into 1-inch chunks, blanch in boiling, salted water for 1 minute, then drain well. Melt butter in a pan, add spring onions (or chopped onion). Cover and cook for 1 minute. Add cucumber, season. Cover and cook for 5-6 minutes or until just tender, occasionally shaking pan gently. Garnish with fresh mint.
Watchpoint Do not overcook or cucumber will become watery and tasteless.

Baked (jacket) potatoes

1 large potato per person
salt
pat of butter per person
parsley (optional)

Method

Well scrub large, even-size potatoes and roll them in salt. Bake for 1½ hours (or until they give when pressed) in an oven at 375°F or Mark 4. Make cross-cuts on top of each potato and squeeze to enlarge cuts. Put a pat of butter and sprig of parsley in centre ; serve at once.

Sauté potatoes

$1\frac{1}{2}$ lb potatoes
2 tablespoons oil
1 oz butter
salt and pepper
1 dessertspoon chopped parsley

Method

Scrub potatoes and boil in their skins until very tender. Then drain, peel and slice. After heating a frying pan, put in oil and when this is hot add the butter. Slip in all the potatoes at once, add seasoning and cook (sauté) until golden-brown and crisp, yet buttery, occasionally turning the contents of the pan. Draw aside, check seasoning, and add parsley. Serve in a very hot dish.

Lyonnaise potatoes

Method

Slice and fry one onion until brown, then remove from pan and sauté the potatoes as in the previous recipe. When these are brown, add the cooked onion slices.

The Lyonnais district of France is renowned for its potatoes and onions, amongst other excellent foodstuffs and special regional dishes.

▶

Vegetables to serve with grills continued

Chip potatoes

2 lb even-size potatoes (weight after peeling)
deep fat, or oil (for frying)
salt

Deep fat bath, or pan, and basket

Method

Square off the ends and sides of the potatoes, then cut down into $\frac{1}{2}$-inch thick slices, then into thick fingers. Soak in cold water for about 30 minutes, then drain. Wrap potatoes in absorbent paper or a cloth and leave for 20-30 minutes.

Heat the fat or oil, which should not come more than two-thirds of the way up the sides of the pan. Dip in the frying basket (this prevents food sticking). Put potatoes in the basket (out of the fat) ; when the fat reaches the right temperature (350°F), gently lower basket into it. If you don't have a frying thermometer, drop in a finger of potato ; if this rises to the surface of the fat straight away and starts to bubble gently, the fat is ready.

Fry gently until the potatoes are just soft (pierce one with the point of a knife to test) but not coloured. Lift out and drain. They can be left like this for a short time before the final frying.

Reheat the fat to 400°F (or oil to 360-375°F). Carefully lower in the basket of potatoes and fry to a deep golden-brown. Drain chips well on absorbent paper, turn into a hot dish for serving and sprinkle with salt. When cool, drain fat through dry muslin, cover and store for future use.

On the first frying, chips are cooked until just soft, drained and set aside

After second frying in hotter fat, drain chips and sprinkle with salt

Brochettes of kidney

Allow one skewer per person and for each skewer the following ingredients :

2 lambs kidneys
2 or 3 squares of lambs liver
boiled rice (for serving)
chopped parsley (to garnish)

For marinade
$2\frac{1}{2}$ fl oz olive oil
2-3 tablespoons red wine
few sprigs of thyme
salt
pepper (ground from mill)

Method

Skin and split kidneys (see page 57), cut the liver into $1\text{-}1\frac{1}{2}$ inch squares and remove the ducts. Marinate the liver and kidneys in the mixture of oil and red wine, adding seasoning and the thyme. Leave for 2-3 hours.

Thread the kidneys and liver alternately on to skewers and grill for 6-8 minutes, moistening with the marinade throughout the cooking time.

Serve brochettes on a bed of boiled rice and sprinkle with chopped parsley.

Threading the marinated liver and kidneys alternately on to skewers

Savoury butters to accompany grills

When these mixtures are made, pat into balls with butter 'hands' (wooden shaping boards), or spread a $\frac{1}{4}$ - $\frac{1}{2}$ inch thick on greaseproof paper and chill. Then cut into small round or square pats before using. The quantities given are enough for 4 people.

Anchovy butter

2 oz unsalted butter
4 anchovy fillets (soaked in milk to remove excess salt)
black pepper (ground from mill)
anchovy essence

Method

Soften the butter on a plate with a palette knife and then crush or pound the anchovies, adding these to the butter with ground pepper and enough essence to strengthen the flavour and give a delicate pink colour.

Serve with mutton, chops or cutlets, and fish.

Orange butter

2 oz unsalted butter
grated rind of ½ an orange and 1 teaspoon juice
1 teaspoon tomato purée
salt and pepper

Method

Soften the butter on a plate with a palette knife, and then add other ingredients, seasoning to taste.

Serve chilled, in pats, with lamb cutlets, steaks and fish.

Maître d'hôtel butter

2 oz unsalted butter
1 dessertspoon chopped parsley
few drops of lemon juice
salt and pepper

Method

Soften the butter on a plate with a palette knife, then add parsley, lemon juice and seasoning to taste.

Serve chilled, in pats, with steaks, mixed grills and fish.

Parsley butter

½ oz butter
1 teaspoon chopped parsley
dash of Worcestershire sauce, or squeeze of lemon juice

Method

Melt the butter in a pan and, when light and brown, add the chopped parsley and Worcestershire sauce or lemon juice. Blend together and then pour sauce over the meat.

Chutney, garlic, mustard or tomato butters

Other savoury butters are made in the same way using 2 oz unsalted butter with either pounded chutney, crushed garlic, 1 dessertspoon French mustard, or tomato purée.

Sauté and fried dishes

Sautéing is advanced work and is an important method of cooking, calling for care and a certain amount of judgment. This comes with practice. Meat, poultry and game are used for a sauté and must be young, tender and of best quality. A sauté is a quick dish to make and good for entertaining as it can be kept waiting without spoiling.

To sauté, fry lightly pieces of meat to seal in juices. Add a small quantity of strong stock, with or without wine. It should come barely level with meat or joints in pan and may at this point be lightly thickened.

When cooking is completed the sauce should be rich and concentrated with just enough to allow 2-3 tablespoons per person. To achieve this, a sauté pan (similar to a large deep frying pan but with straight sides and a lid) should be used. The wide base allows room for browning and for quick reduction of sauce. The lid helps to slow up this reduction, if necessary, and ensures the cooking of the meat. If you haven't a proper sauté pan, use your deepest frying pan with a pan lid or plate as a cover.

When the meat is arranged in the serving dish, you must use your own judgment as to whether the sauce should be further reduced to strengthen the flavour and thicken it a little more.

Watchpoint Care must be taken not to over-reduce, as this will give a harsh taste. If the flavour is right but the sauce is too thin, thicken with a tiny quantity of arrowroot mixed with a little cold water.

In more advanced recipes a previously-made sauce is added towards end of cooking, the sauté taking its name from the sauce or any other ingredient or garnish.

To sauté is also a term used to describe cooking briskly in a small quantity of butter and/or oil and is particularly suitable for vegetables. Freshly boiled potatoes are delicious sautéd in butter until crisp and golden-brown in appearance, with a soft and buttery taste. Cold cooked leftover potatoes, while making a very good 'pan fry', are not the same thing.

Vegetables which can be sautéd raw, with a lid on the pan, include jerusalem artichokes, chicory, marrow, celery and leeks. They should be thickly sliced and cooked in butter with little or no liquid. They do not colour, but retain all their flavour and cook comparatively quickly in 7-10 minutes.

Lamb cutlets Reform

2 lb best end neck of lamb (chined)
1 tablespoon seasoned flour
1 egg (beaten)
5-6 tablespoons dried white breadcrumbs (see page 152)
2 oz lean cooked ham (finely chopped)
4 tablespoons oil
1 oz butter

For garnish
1 medium-size carrot
3 gherkins
1 egg white (steamed)
3 firm white button mushrooms
2-3 tablespoons stock
$\frac{1}{2}$ oz butter
salt and pepper

For sauce
1 teaspoon redcurrant jelly (see page 29)
1 tablespoon port
$\frac{1}{2}$ pint demi-glace sauce (see page 153)
a speck of cayenne pepper

This dish was created at the Reform Club in London by Alexis Soyer, their first chef.

Method

Divide the meat into cutlets, trim well and roll in seasoned flour ; brush with beaten egg and roll in the crumbs mixed with the chopped ham. Now prepare the garnish. Cut the carrot in thin strips and cook in boiling salted water until tender, then drain. Cut the gherkins and egg white in pieces all the same size. Wash and trim the mushrooms and cut across in slices $\frac{1}{4}$ inch thick. Heat all the garnish together in a little stock and toss in the butter and seasoning just before it is required for use.

To make the sauce : melt the redcurrant jelly in the port, add the demi-glace sauce, bring to the boil and season with the tiniest amount of cayenne pepper.

Heat the oil and butter together and fry cutlets until golden-brown. Drain the cutlets, arrange in a circle on a hot serving dish, pile the garnish in the centre and pour the sauce round.

Lamb cutlets Tante Elise

8 small lamb cutlets
1 oz butter
½ lb pork sausage meat
1 medium can pâté de foie
large piece of pig's caul (membrane)
1 shallot (finely chopped)
2 oz mushrooms (washed, trimmed and chopped)
salt and pepper
¾ oz plain flour
½ pint jellied stock (see page 155)

Method

Bat out the cutlets, melt the butter in a frying pan and cook the cutlets very gently for 2-3 minutes on each side, just enough to firm and whiten the flesh. Remove from the pan, and allow to cool. Mix the sausage meat and pâté together and then cover both sides of the cutlets, reshaping very carefully. Wrap a piece of pig's caul around each cutlet. Reheat the fat in the frying pan, put in the cutlets and sauté carefully for about 5 minutes on each side. Lift on to an entrée dish and keep in oven (325°F or Mark 3) while preparing the sauce.

Add the shallot to the frying pan, cook for 1 minute, then add the mushrooms, season and cook carefully to dry off the mixture. Then blend in the flour and the stock ; stir until boiling and simmer for 3-5 minutes. Spoon sauce over cutlets ; serve.

A cutlet bat is used to flatten the lamb cutlets before they are cooked

Before further cooking, cutlets are covered with the pâté mixture

Lamb cutlets au fromage

- 2 lb best end of neck of lamb cutlets
- 2 oz butter (melted)
- 8 tablespoons fresh white breadcrumbs
- 2 oz Gruyère cheese (finely grated)
- 2 oz clarified butter, or 2 tablespoons oil (for frying)
- 2 lb spinach
- $\frac{1}{2}$ oz butter

For sauce

- 1 onion (finely chopped)
- $\frac{3}{4}$ oz butter
- 1 dessertspoon plain flour
- 1 medium-size can ($\frac{1}{2}$ pint) tomatoes
- 2 caps of pimiento (chopped)
- pinch of ground mace
- bouquet garni (containing 2 strips of pared lemon rind)
- 1 teaspoon tomato purée
- $\frac{1}{4}$ pint stock (see page 155)
- salt and pepper
- granulated sugar (to taste)

Method

Trim cutlets, scraping bones well. Dip in melted butter, then into a mixture of grated cheese and crumbs ; press this on well, then repeat the process so that each cutlet is covered twice. Set cutlets aside.

To prepare sauce ; cook onion in the butter, stir in flour, then add remaining ingredients. Season, then simmer the sauce for 25 30 minutes until it is reduced. Press it through a strainer, return it to the pan and continue to simmer until it is syrupy.

Cook the spinach in plenty of boiling salted water for about 5 minutes, drain it, then press between two plates to remove all the water. Sauté the cutlets in the butter or oil for 7 minutes. Toss the spinach in the $\frac{1}{2}$ oz butter and season well. Pour a small quantity of the sauce on the serving dish, arrange the cutlets in a circle and fill the middle with the spinach.

Serve the remaining sauce separately.

Noisettes of lamb Henry IV

2 lb best end of neck of lamb (boned)
salt and pepper
1 teaspoon fresh thyme and marjoram (mixed and chopped), or large pinch of dried herbs
1 dessertspoon chopped parsley
6-8 slices of stale bread
deep fat (for frying)
1½-2 lb spinach, or 12 oz packet of frozen leaf spinach
1 tablespoon melted butter, or oil
½ oz butter (for spinach)
1 glass sherry
1 sherry glass stock (see page 155)
¼ teaspoon meat, or vegetable, extract

To finish
½ oz butter
grate of nutmeg
potato croquettes (see right)
béarnaise sauce (see page 154)

Method

Season lamb, dust with herbs and roll up. Tie with fine string at 1-1½ inch intervals and cut between the string to give noisettes (see photograph opposite). Cut rounds of bread to fit noisettes, fry rounds in deep fat until golden-brown.

Cook the spinach in plenty of boiling salted water, drain and press leaves between two plates to remove all the moisture (or cook frozen spinach as directed on packet).

Prepare the potato croquettes, keep warm, and prepare the béarnaise sauce, set aside.

Grill or sauté the noisettes in the butter (or oil), allowing about 3 minutes on each side, and dish up on the croûtes of fried bread ; arrange these in a circle on a hot serving dish.

Pour off the fat and deglaze the pan with the sherry and stock, add the meat or vegetable extract and simmer for 4-5 minutes; pour the sauce into a gravy boat for serving.

Toss the spinach in butter until it is piping hot, season and add nutmeg. Pile the spinach in the middle of the dish, put a teaspoon of béarnaise sauce on each noisette and surround with the potato croquettes, or serve separately.

Making noisettes of lamb by cutting the rolled meat between string

Potato croquettes

Pass 1 lb boiled potatoes through a wire sieve, return to pan, beat in ½ oz butter, 1 egg yolk, 2 tablespoons hot milk and seasoning. Divide into cork-shaped pieces, roll in seasoned flour, brush with beaten egg, roll in dried white breadcrumbs. Fry in butter or oil until golden-brown.

Hungarian grenadins of veal

4 grenadins
1 aubergine
2 oz butter
1 tablespoon seasoned flour
1 shallot (finely chopped)
1 teaspoon paprika pepper
2-3 tablespoons white wine
¼ pint double cream
salt and pepper
½ pint mornay sauce (see page 154)
1 dessertspoon grated Parmesan cheese

A grenadin is a small thick 'nut' of meat (weighing approximately 3 oz), which is cut from the boned loin or fillet of veal.

Method

Cut the aubergine into neat slices, score with a knife, sprinkle lightly with salt and leave for 30 minutes. Drain off any liquid and wipe dry with absorbent paper, then dust with a little flour. Melt the butter in a sauté pan and fry the aubergine slices for about 1 minute on each side; remove from the pan and keep warm. Then dust the grenadins with the seasoned flour and cook for about 3 minutes on each side in the same pan, remove and keep warm. Add the shallot to the pan and cook slowly for 2 minutes, then add paprika and continue cooking a further 2 minutes. Pour on the wine and reduce by half. Pour in the cream, season, bring sauce to the boil and then keep it on one side.

Place the grenadins in a serving dish with the slices of aubergine on the top, coat with the mornay sauce, sprinkle with cheese and brown under the grill. Reheat the paprika sauce and pour it round the dish.

Veal scaloppine à la crème

3-4 veal escalopes
1 oz butter
1 small onion (finely chopped)
1 small glass sherry
1 dessertspoon plain flour
$\frac{1}{4}$ pint stock (see page 156)
2 oz button mushrooms (sliced thinly)
salt and pepper
2 tablespoons double cream

Method

Cut escalopes (thin pieces of meat cut from leg or fillet) in half to form scaloppine (small escalopes). Heat a sauté pan, drop in the butter and, while still foaming, put in the pieces of veal. Cook briskly for 3-4 minutes, turning once, remove from the pan, add chopped onion and cook for 1-2 minutes ; then pour on sherry.

Boil sherry to reduce a little, then draw aside. Stir in flour and stock, bring to the boil, add mushrooms and veal, and season. Cover the pan and simmer meat gently for 8-10 minutes. Taste for seasoning, add the cream and reheat without boiling.

Veal chops monarque

4 veal chops
2 oz butter
4 oz mushrooms (washed and finely chopped)
2 oz Gruyère cheese (grated)
salt
pepper (ground from mill)
4 oz small pasta shells
$\frac{1}{4}$ oz butter
2 oz ham (cut in strips)
1 wineglass port

Method

Melt 1 oz of the butter and sauté the chops slowly on one side until golden-brown; remove from pan. Put the mushrooms into the pan and cook quickly to drive off all the moisture. Reduce the heat, add the cheese and stir over gentle heat until it melts. Season to taste. Spread this mixture on the cooked side of the chops, put them back into the pan with the remaining butter and cook the undersides for 2-3 minutes.

Put the pan into oven, pre-set at 400°F or Mark 6, for 6-8 minutes to glaze the top.

Meanwhile cook the pasta in boiling water until just tender, drain and refresh, return to the pan and heat with $\frac{1}{4}$ oz butter, pepper ground from the mill and ham. Take up chops and arrange in a serving dish; pour the port into pan and bring to the boil, scraping the bottom and sides well. Strain this sauce over chops; garnish with pasta.

Mushroom and cheese mixture is spread on the cooked side of the veal chops monarque

Wiener schnitzel

4-5 thin escalopes (measuring about 5 inches by 3 inches)
seasoned flour
1 egg beaten (seasoned and 2-3 drops of oil added)
dry white breadcrumbs (see page 152)
clarified butter, or a mixture of oil and butter (for frying)

For garnish
1 lemon (sliced)
capers
gherkins (sliced)

To finish
1-2 oz butter
juice of 1 lemon
chopped parsley

Method

Roll the escalopes in seasoned flour, shake, brush with egg and roll in the crumbs, pressing them on well.

Heat the butter in a large frying pan, put in the escalopes and fry over a moderate to slow heat for about 7-10 minutes, turning once only. Place veal on a hot, flat dish, garnishing the middle of each schnitzel with a slice of lemon topped with capers and gherkins. Keep warm while preparing the butter.

Wipe out the pan, reheat and drop in the 1-2 oz butter. Cook to a noisette (until nut-brown), add lemon juice and pour over the escalopes just before sending to table. Dust with chopped parsley and serve at once.

Escalopes of veal sauté à l'anglaise

5 veal escalopes
2 tablespoons seasoned flour
1 egg (beaten)
1 cup fresh white breadcrumbs
2 oz clarified butter (see page 157)

For garnish
1 bundle of asparagus
5 slices of ham
2 ½ oz butter
juice of ½ small lemon
salt and pepper

Method

Trim escalopes, dip in seasoned flour, brush with beaten egg, then coat with the crumbs, pressing them on well. Set aside.

Trim asparagus and cut off the stalks to give 2-3 inch long tips. Retie in bundles and cook, tips upwards, in plenty of boiling, salted water until tender. Then drain and keep warm. Sauté slices of ham for 1-2 minutes in ½ oz of butter for the garnish, keep warm.

Heat a large frying or sauté pan, put in the clarified butter, add the escalopes and sauté gently for 3-4 minutes on each side, turning once only, until golden-brown. Take up escalopes and arrange in a serving dish, laying a piece of ham in between each escalope. Arrange the asparagus tips in the centre. Keep the dish warm.

Wipe out sauté pan and reheat. Drop in remaining butter, colour to a noisette (nut-brown), then add the lemon juice with seasoning ; pour over the escalopes while still foaming and serve at once.

Above : pouring sauce over the garnished veal escalopes
Below : finished dish of escalopes of veal sauté à l'anglaise

Beef Stroganov

$1\frac{1}{2}$ lb fillet of beef
2-3 onions (sliced)
butter (for frying)
6 oz mushrooms (sliced)
salt and pepper
1 cup soured cream, or fresh double cream soured with juice of $\frac{1}{2}$ lemon

Method

Cut the fillet into strips about the size of your small finger and set aside. Fry the onions slowly in butter until golden-brown, lift out with a slice and keep warm. Fry mushrooms and keep warm with the onions. Increase the heat and fry the steak very quickly for 3-4 minutes on each side, taking care that the juice does not run. To avoid this, fry the meat in two lots so that the temperature is not lowered too much. Return all meat to the pan, season well, add the onions and mushrooms and shake up over the heat. Pour in the soured cream, bring quickly to the boil and serve with plainly boiled rice.

Beef Stroganov is ideal for cooking in a chafing dish, if you have one

Beef sauté chasseur

2 lb porterhouse steak, or skirt (cut in one piece)
3 shallots, or 1 small onion
1 clove of garlic
2 tablespoons oil
1 $\frac{1}{2}$ oz butter
1 tablespoon plain flour
$\frac{1}{2}$-$\frac{3}{4}$ pint jellied brown stock (see page 155)
salt and pepper
$\frac{1}{2}$ lb button mushrooms
2 wineglasses white wine
1 dessertspoon tomato purée
1 tablespoon chopped parsley (to garnish)

Method

Cut the meat into 2-inch squares. Chop the shallots (or onion) and garlic very finely. Heat a sauté pan or shallow stew-pan, add the oil and, when hot, drop in 1 oz butter ; fry the meat a few pieces at a time until nicely brown on both sides, then remove it from the pan. Reduce the heat, add the shallot and garlic and cook slowly until soft, dust in the flour and continue cooking to a rich russet-brown. Draw pan aside, blend in the stock, then replace on heat and stir until boiling. Return the meat to the pan, season, cover the pan and simmer until tender (about 45 minutes).

Wash and trim the mushrooms, quarter them or leave whole, depending on their size. Heat a pan, drop in $\frac{1}{2}$ oz butter and mushrooms and cook quickly for about 2 minutes, tip on the wine and boil hard until reduced by half ; stir in the tomato purée. Add the mushroom mixture to the meat and continue cooking for about 10 minutes. Turn into a hot serving dish and dust with chopped parsley. Serve with sauté potatoes (see page 63) and leaf spinach.

Tournedos Clamart

5 tournedos
5 slices of bread for croûtes (about $\frac{1}{4}$ inch thick)
2 oz butter
3 tablespoons oil
1$\frac{1}{2}$ lb potatoes (for parisienne potatoes)
1-2 tablespoons chopped parsley

For garnish
5 artichoke 'fonds', or hearts (fresh, or canned)
2 oz butter
1$\frac{1}{2}$ lb peas ($\frac{1}{2}$ pint shelled)
little mint and granulated sugar (for cooking)
5 button mushrooms (washed and trimmed)
1 wineglass white wine
$\frac{1}{2}$ pint demi-glace sauce (see page 153)

Method

Prepare the parisienne potatoes by scooping out potato balls with a cutter, plain boiling them, tossing in $\frac{1}{2}$ oz butter and then chopped parsley. Keep hot.

To prepare garnish : drain canned artichoke hearts and warm gently in $\frac{1}{2}$ oz of the butter. For the preparation of fresh artichokes, see left.

Simmer the peas in salted water with mint and sugar for flavour, drain, add a nut of butter and keep hot. Cook the mushrooms in $\frac{1}{2}$ oz of the butter.

Trim the bread for croûtes to same size as tournedos, heat $\frac{1}{2}$ oz butter and the oil and fry croûtes. Wipe out the pan, reheat it, drop in about 1 oz butter ; fry the tournedos for 3 minutes on each side, put a mushroom on each one, place on croûtes and arrange in a serving dish. Keep hot.

Tip the wine into the pan and boil until reduced to half the quantity. Add demi-glace sauce and simmer for 1 minute. Stir

Tournedos Clamart : frying meat in butter for 3 minutes on each side

Preparation of fresh artichoke hearts

Mix 4 tablespoons of flour to a paste with 2 pints of water, add the juice of $\frac{1}{2}$ lemon and bring to the boil.

Remove the leaves one by one from the raw artichokes and then remove the inedible 'choke' with the point of a teaspoon.

Place the artichoke 'fonds' in the boiling liquid and then simmer until tender (about 35-45 minutes).

Watchpoint Do not remove the artichokes from the pan until you are ready to serve them, as they quickly turn black.

in remaining butter (about $\frac{1}{2}$ oz), a small piece at a time, then spoon over the tournedos.

Arrange the artichoke hearts between the tournedos, fill artichokes with peas and pile the hot parisienne potatoes in the centre of dish.

Tournedos Clamart are served on croûtes and garnished with button mushrooms, parisienne potatoes and peas on artichoke hearts

Crumbed kidneys

8 lambs kidneys
1 oz butter (melted)
1 egg (beaten)
1 cup dry white breadcrumbs (see page 152)
2 oz butter (for frying)
8 rashers streaky bacon
1 tablespoon chopped parsley
hot buttered toast

Method

Skin and core kidneys (see photographs and page 57), partially split and open them ; thread on skewers, allowing 2 kidneys per skewer. Brush with the butter and egg, then roll in the crumbs. Heat a sauté, or deep frying, pan, put in 1 oz of the butter and then kidneys. Sauté until nicely brown, allowing 3$\frac{1}{2}$ minutes on each side. Take out and keep warm. Wipe out the pan, put in the rest of the butter and fry the rashers of bacon in this, then take out. Return kidneys to pan, scatter on the parsley and turn in the butter in the pan, then arrange the fried bacon on the top of the skewered kidneys.

For serving, push kidneys off skewers on to a piece of hot buttered toast, or on to a hot dish or plate.

Note : if preferred, kidneys may be cooked without egging and crumbing.

In this case thread the pieces of bacon on to the skewer with the kidneys. Then sauté in butter over brisk heat, allowing about 3 minutes on each side. Dish up the kidneys, melt a little extra butter in the dish, add the chopped parsley and a good squeeze of lemon juice to make a sauce. Serve piping hot on buttered toast.

Kidneys Turbigo

5 lambs kidneys
12-18 pickling onions
2 oz butter
$\frac{1}{4}$ lb chipolata sausages
$\frac{1}{4}$ lb button mushrooms (quartered)
1 dessertspoon plain flour
1 teaspoon tomato purée
1 tablespoon sherry
7 $\frac{1}{2}$ fl oz brown stock (see page 155)
1 bayleaf
salt and pepper
2 slices of stale bread (for croûtes)
oil (for frying croûtes)
parsley (chopped)

Method

Blanch the onions and drain. Skin the kidneys, cut in half lengthways and core (see photographs and page 57).

Heat a sauté or deep frying pan, drop in the butter and, when it is foaming, put in the kidneys and sauté briskly until evenly browned.

Lift out kidneys and put in chipolata sausages, lower the heat and cook until brown on all sides. Take them out, add the onions and mushrooms, shake over a brisk heat for 2-3 minutes, then draw pan aside.

Stir in the flour, tomato purée, sherry and stock and bring to the boil ; add the bayleaf and season. Slice sausages and kidneys and put in the pan. Cover and simmer gently for 20-25 minutes, or until tender.

To make the croûtes, cut bread into triangular pieces and fry in a little hot oil until golden-brown.

Serve the kidneys and sausages surrounded with croûtes and sprinkled with parsley.

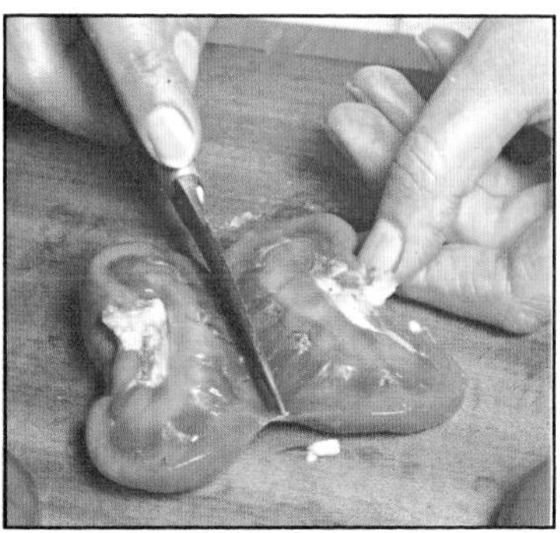

Removing the skin from a lamb's kidney and (right) halving the kidney before cutting out its core

Below : kidneys Turbigo surrounded with triangular croûtes of bread and sprinkled with chopped parsley

Fried liver with orange

6 good slices of calves liver
2 tablespoons plain flour
seasoning (salt, pepper, dry mustard, cayenne pepper)
2 oz butter
1 onion (finely sliced)
2 cloves of garlic (crushed)
5 tablespoons red wine
5 tablespoons strong stock (see **page 155**)
1 tablespoon chopped parsley and thyme
1 orange (cut in thin slices)
extra butter, or oil (for frying)

For pilaf
1 oz butter
1 onion (finely chopped)
5 oz long grain rice
$\frac{3}{4}$ pint veal, or chicken, stock (see **page 155**)
salt and pepper
little cheese (grated)

Method

First prepare pilaf. Melt $\frac{3}{4}$ oz butter in flameproof dish, add onion, cover and cook slowly until soft but not coloured. Add rice and sauté for 3-4 minutes stirring all the time. Pour on the stock, season and bring to the boil.

Cover with a tightly fitting lid and cook in the oven at 350°F or Mark 4 for 20-30 minutes, or until tender. Mix in the remaining butter with a fork and stir in a little grated cheese.

Dust the slices of liver lightly with seasoned flour. Heat 1 oz butter in a pan and cook liver 3-4 minutes on each side. Put in a serving dish and keep warm.

Melt the remaining butter in the pan, add the onion and garlic and cook until onion is soft and golden-brown. Moisten with the wine and stock, add herbs and simmer for 1 minute. Pour the sauce over the liver.

Cut the orange in thin slices (leaving on the skin). Sprinkle well with sugar and brown quickly on both sides in hot butter or oil.

Garnish liver with orange slices and serve pilaf separately.

Sauté of liver italienne

6 slices of calves liver
3-4 oz butter
1 medium-size onion (finely chopped)
3 oz mushrooms (finely chopped)
$\frac{1}{2}$ wineglass white wine
$\frac{1}{2}$ wineglass stock (see page 155)
1 good teaspoon tomato purée
3 oz sliced, cooked ham (diced, or chopped)
1 tablespoon plain flour
salt and pepper
pinch of ground mace, or nutmeg
1 tablespoon mixed fresh herbs (parsley, tarragon and chervil) — chopped

Method

Heat about $1\frac{1}{2}$ oz of the butter in a saucepan, add the onion and cook gently for 2-3 minutes. Then add the mushrooms, increase heat and cook quickly for 3-4 minutes. Add the wine and boil to reduce a little. Stir in the stock and tomato purée, cover and cook gently for 10 minutes. Then add the ham, and leave to simmer gently.

Put the flour, sifted with salt, pepper and spice, on to a plate and roll the slices of liver in this. Melt rest of butter in a frying pan, put in the liver and fry for 3-4 minutes on each side, shaking the pan frequently. Put on a serving dish, add herbs to sauce and pour over the liver.

Pork fillet sauté normande

$1\frac{1}{2}$ lb pork fillet / tenderloin
1 oz butter
1 medium-size onion (finely sliced)
1 dessert apple
1 tablespoon plain flour
1 wineglass dry cider
$\frac{1}{4}$ pint stock (see page 155)
salt and pepper
2 tablespoons double cream

Method

Brown pork fillet on all sides in the butter, remove from the pan, add the onion and cook for 2-3 minutes. Peel, core and slice the apple, add to the pan and continue cooking until both onion and apple are golden-brown. Stir in the flour, cider and stock and bring to the boil. Put the fillet back in the pan, season, cover the pan and simmer gently for 45-50 minutes until meat is tender. This can be done on top of the stove or in the oven at 350°F or Mark 4.

Remove the meat from the sauce, cut in slanting, $1\frac{1}{2}$-inch slices and place on a hot serving dish. Strain the sauce, reheat and then stir in the cream. Taste for seasoning and spoon over the meat.

Pork chops ardennaise

- 4-5 lean loin pork chops
- 2 thick gammon rashers (about 8 oz in all)
- 2 wineglasses white wine
- 3 shallots (finely chopped)
- salt
- pepper (ground from mill)
- 2 tablespoons plain flour
- 2 oz butter
- $\frac{1}{4}$ pint double cream
- 1 teaspoon French mustard
- 1 tablespoon chopped parsley

Method

Remove rind from the gammon rashers, cut them into small squares or julienne strips. Place in a bowl and cover with the wine and shallots and leave to soak for about 30 minutes. Then drain gammon and shallots and reserve them and the wine separately. Lightly season the pork chops and roll them in the flour.

Heat the butter over a moderate heat and gently fry the chops for 6-7 minutes on each side. Add the shallots and gammon, continue cooking for 2-3 minutes, then pour on the reserved wine and the cream. Simmer gently for 10-12 minutes.

Take up the chops and arrange them on a hot serving dish. Reduce the sauce a little in the pan, add the French mustard and parsley, taste for seasoning and spoon this sauce over the chops. Serve with plainly boiled potatoes, and braised chicory with orange (see page 88).

Braised chicory with orange

1 lb chicory
1-2 oz butter
salt
pepper (ground from mill)
rind and juice of 1 orange

Method

Wipe the chicory, remove any damaged outer leaves and scoop out the core at the bottom.

Butter a casserole, put in the chicory, season and add the rind and juice of the orange. Cover with a buttered paper and lid and cook in a moderate oven, pre-set at 350°F or Mark 4, for about 1½ hours.

Shami kababs

1 lb lean mutton, or beef (very finely minced)
1 medium-size onion (very finely chopped)
1 green chilli (seeds removed and flesh chopped)
1 clove of garlic (crushed with salt)
1 medium-size potato (peeled, boiled and mashed)
1 teaspoon garam masala
1 dessertspoon thick infusion of tamarind (see below)
1-inch piece fresh ginger (grated)
1 teaspoon salt
2 oz fat, or melted butter (for frying)

8-10 skewers (optional)

This dish is of Indian origin

Method

Mix all the ingredients (except the fat) together. Shape into balls the size of large walnuts and flatten slightly. Heat the fat and fry the balls gently until they are brown and cooked right through.

Alternatively these may be slipped carefully on to long greased skewers, basted with melted butter and grilled until they are brown and cooked through. Set them a little apart from one another on the skewers and turn and baste once or twice as they cook. Serve with rice and chutneys.

Tamarind (imli) : the pod of the tamarind tree is used with a little sugar (gur) to give a sweet-acid effect. A piece about the size of an egg is added to ½ teacup of boiling water, left to infuse for 10 minutes, and then squeezed through muslin.

Meat pies and puddings

It is a long time since anyone ate a pie as ambitious as the one containing four and twenty blackbirds ; but meat pies on a more modest scale have retained their popularity.

One main advantage of encasing meat in a pie crust is, of course, economy. A delicious pastry case and good, rich gravy can turn a small portion of meat into a substantial meal ; or it can turn a joint of ample quantity into a sumptuous meal of magnificent proportions.

In the old days, the economy stretched to the method of cooking, too, for a meat pie could be baked in the oven alongside any number of other dishes. Moreover it required little or no attention while cooking, whereas a joint roasting on the open fire demanded constant watchfulness from the cook, as well as an assistant to stand and turn the spit.

Pies used to be a popular choice for meals that had to travel — whether for an afternoon's picnic or for a journey of several days on horse or foot. This old custom is reflected in more modern habits ; we do not often carry large hot pies away from home, but cold ones, or slices of larger ones, particularly pork and veal, are often chosen for picnic meals, while small hot pies and pasties are a popular buy as a lunchtime snack.

When making pastry for meat pies, follow the general rules below, and turn to the Appendix for basic pastry recipes not given in the text.

General rules for making pastry

1 Work in a cool, airy room. Plan to make the pastry before the kitchen becomes warm from other cooking because a damp, warm atmosphere is disastrous.

2 Use fresh, fine-sifted, plain flour, firm but not hard fat and ice-cold water for mixing.

3 Handle flour and fat lightly but firmly. When rubbing fat into the flour, keep lifting it up and crumbling the mixture between your fingers. This movement helps to aerate the pastry. Shake the bowl after 1-2 minutes to bring the larger lumps of fat to the surface and to show you how much more rubbing-in is necessary.

4 Make sure the correct amount of water is added. This may vary a little with the quality of the flour. Too dry a mixture makes the pastry difficult to handle ; too wet a dough will shrink and lose shape while baking, and also makes for tough, hard pastry.

5 A marble slab, or slate shelf, is ideal for rolling out pastry because it is smooth, solid and cool ; otherwise keep a board specially for the purpose (laminated plastic is cool). Always scrape a slab or board thoroughly before rolling out new pastry to remove any dough that may have stuck and which might cause further sticking. Use a minimum amount of flour for dusting when rolling, otherwise too much will go into the pastry and spoil it. A heavy, plain, wooden rolling pin is best, without handles.

6 Chill made pastry for about 30 minutes, or leave it in a cool place. This removes any elasticity which may cause shrinkage round the edge of the dish.

7 It is essential when baking pastry to pre-set the oven to the required temperature. The immediate heat sets the pastry in its correct shape and makes it possible to control the exact amount of cooking time.

Note : when terms such as '8 oz of pastry', or 'an 8 oz quantity of pastry' are used, this means the amount obtained by using 8 oz of flour, not 8 oz of prepared dough.

Fillet of pork 'en croûte'

3 large pork fillets (about 2½-3 lb in all)
4 oz cooked ham (sliced)
8 oz puff pastry (see page 154)
watercress (to garnish)

For mushroom stuffing
1 medium-size onion (chopped)
1 oz butter
¼ lb mushrooms (finely chopped)
1 teaspoon chopped parsley
1 teaspoon chopped sage
4 oz cooked ham (chopped)
2-3 tablespoons fresh white breadcrumbs
salt and pepper
trimmings of pork fillets (minced)
beaten egg

Method

Trim fillets and carefully split them lengthways. Set the oven at 400°F or Mark 6.

To prepare the stuffing : soften the onion in the butter. Wash the mushrooms in salted water, chop finely and add to the pan with the herbs. Cover and cook for about 5 minutes.

Draw pan off heat, add the chopped ham, breadcrumbs and seasoning, then turn into a bowl to cool. Work in the minced pork trimmings and enough beaten egg to bind. Fill this stuffing into the fillets, truss or tie neatly, then roast in pre-set hot oven for 1-1¼ hours, until meat is tender. Baste meat frequently.

Leave the meat to go quite cold, then remove the string and roll the meat in the sliced ham.

Roll out the pastry to a large rectangle and trim the sides to give yourself enough pieces to cut fleurons (crescents) for decoration. Turn the pastry over so that the rolled surface, the best side of the pastry, is on the outside when baked.

Set the meat on the pastry, dampen the outside edges and roll meat up in it like a swiss roll ; tuck in the ends and press firmly. Brush with beaten egg and decorate with fleurons. Lift on to a dampened baking sheet, cook in oven at 425°F or Mark 7, until well browned (about 30 minutes).

Garnish with watercress and serve separately a good brown sauce such as demi-glace sauce (see page 153).

Steak and kidney pie

1½ lb skirt, or sticking, of beef
6 oz ox kidney
salt and pepper
1 tablespoon plain flour
1 shallot, or ½ small onion (finely chopped)
1 teaspoon chopped parsley (optional)
½ pint cold water, or stock (see page 155)
hot water, or stock (to dilute gravy)

For flaky pastry
8 oz plain flour
3 oz lard
3 oz butter
about 8 tablespoons cold water
1 egg (beaten) — to glaze

10-inch long pie dish, pie funnel

A pie funnel supports pastry in centre of the dish and allows meat to be nicely domed without being too tightly packed. Meat, therefore, cooks more evenly and leaves enough liquid in dish to help the stewing of the meat.

It also makes a natural place for a hole in the pastry to allow steam to escape during the long cooking, which stops pastry getting soggy underneath.

The hole is generally camouflaged just before serving with a decoration of pastry leaves around it. (This can be cooked either on the pie, or separately and laid over the hole just before serving.) Or a fine china bird can be inserted into the funnel, like a stopper.

Method

Prepare the flaky pastry (see method, page 154). Well grease the pie dish. Set oven at 425°F or Mark 7.

Cut the steak into 1-inch cubes ; skin and core kidney and cut into pieces ; roll both well in seasoned flour (for this amount of meat add as much salt as you can hold between two fingers and your thumb, and half as much pepper, to the 1 tablespoon of flour).

Place meat in the pie dish, sprinkling each layer with the shallot and parsley, and set the pie funnel in the centre. Pour in the cold water or stock and cover pie with the pastry in the following way.

Roll out pastry ¼ inch thick and cut off a piece large enough to cover and overlap the top of the pie dish ; roll the remainder a little thinner and cut two strips, each ½ inch wide. Damp the edge of the pie dish, press on the strips of pastry and brush with water. Lift the sheet of pastry on your rolling pin and cover the prepared pie.

Watchpoint Do not stretch pastry when covering pie or it will shrink during cooking and slide into the pie dish. When trimming the pastry to fit the dish, lift the pie on one hand and, holding a knife at an angle away from the dish, cut the overlapping pastry in short brisk strokes. To trim in one continuous cut would drag the pastry, spoil the appearance and prevent it rising in good flakes.

Seal the edges of the double thickness of pastry. Scallop the edge (see page 104). Any remaining strips or trimmings of pastry can be used to cut a centre decoration of a rose or thistle, and leaves.

Mix a large pinch of salt into the beaten egg, stir until the salt dissolves and the egg looks darker in colour. Brush this over top of pie (adding salt to beaten egg gives a very brown, shiny gloss to cooked pastry). Arrange the centre decoration, brush pastry with the beaten egg.

Bake 20-30 minutes in the pre-set oven, then cover the pie with a large sheet of damp greaseproof paper, pleating and twisting it under the dish to hold it in place. This prevents the pastry getting too brown and hard during the long cooking which follows. Reduce the oven heat to 325°F or Mark 3 and cook for a further 1½ hours.

To serve : as the gravy in the pie is very strong and concentrated, have ready a small jug of hot stock or water and, when the first portion of pastry is cut, pour in a little to dilute and increase the quantity of gravy for serving.

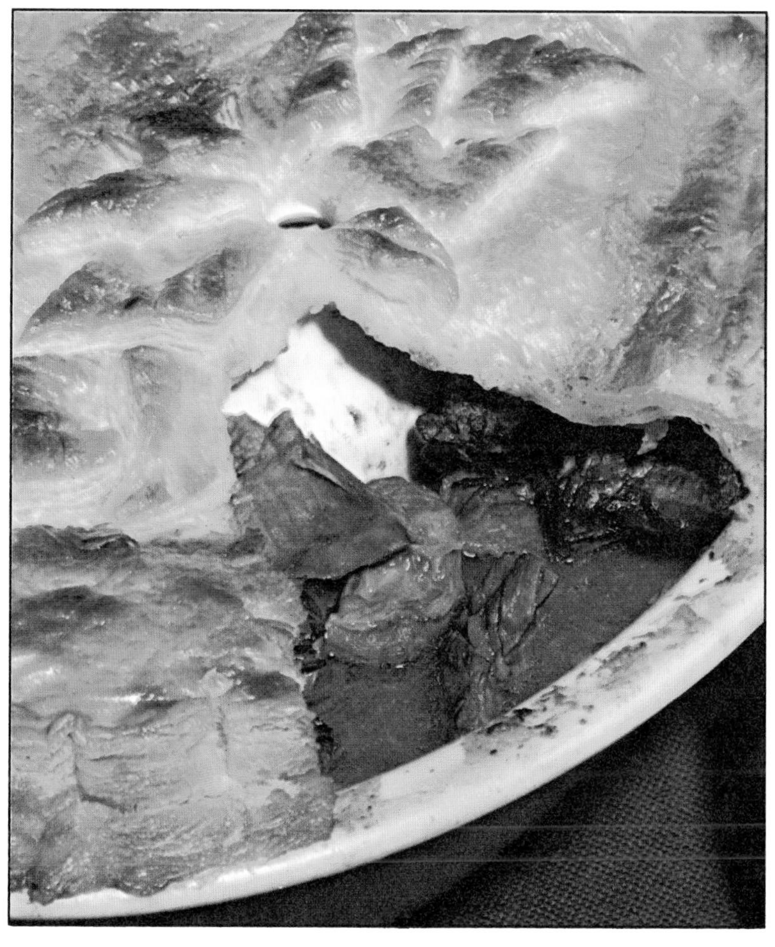

Steak and kidney pudding

$1\frac{1}{2}$ lb skirt, or sticking, of beef
6 oz ox kidney
1 tablespoon seasoned flour
1 small onion (finely chopped)
cold water

For suet crust pastry
8 oz self-raising flour
pinch of salt
6 oz suet
4 fl oz cold water (to mix)

6-inch diameter pudding basin ($1\frac{1}{2}$ pints capacity)

For a particularly light crust 1 oz of the flour can be replaced by the same weight of fresh white breadcrumbs.

Method

Cut the steak and kidney into $\frac{1}{2}$-inch cubes.

To prepare the suet crust pastry : sift the flour with salt into a bowl. If using fresh butcher's suet, remove any skin and chop finely, using a little of the measured flour to prevent it sticking to your knife. Stir the suet into the flour and mix to a firm dough with the cold water.

Grease the basin well. Take two thirds of the pastry and roll out a circle about 1 inch thick.

To make a lining of this crust to fit the basin without creases, first dust centre of pastry with flour, then fold in half and make a deep pleat in the double layer of the pastry at each of the curved, open sides.

Now roll out the folded end to elongate this doubled section of the pastry, open out this 'pocket' you have just made and brush off the surplus flour.

Lift the pastry carefully by putting your fist in the 'pocket' and line into the basin. Work up the thicker part of the pastry with your hands so that it stands about $\frac{1}{2}$-1 inch above the top of the basin. Roll out the remaining third of pastry to a round to fit the top.

Roll the meat in seasoned flour, mix with the onion and fill into the basin ; pour in enough cold water to three-parts fill ; damp the edge of the pastry, put on the lid and roll and pinch edges well together.

Have ready a piece of clean linen cloth, scald by dipping in boiling water and wring out. Flour the underside, make a 1-inch pleat in the middle to allow for rising and lay it over the pudding. Tie round with string and then knot the four corners of the cloth back over the top.

Submerge the basin in a large pan of fast boiling water and boil steadily for 3-4 hours.

To serve, take off the cloth and tie a clean folded napkin round the basin. Serve at the table with a small jug of boiling water. When the first portion of pudding is cut, a little water is poured in to increase and dilute the very rich gravy.

Steak and kidney pudding with a napkin tied round basin, as traditionally served

Beefsteak, pigeon and mushroom pie

2 pigeons
1 oz butter
1½ lb shin of beef (cut into 1-inch squares)
2 pints chicken stock (see page 155)
salt and pepper
½ pint aspic jelly (commercially prepared)
¼ lb flat mushrooms
8 oz flaky, or puff, pastry (see page 154)
1 egg (beaten)
pinch of salt

9-inch long pie dish, pie funnel

Method

Melt the butter in a large stew-pan, add the pigeons and brown slowly. Remove pigeons from the pan, split in half and return to the pan with the squares of beef and the stock. Season with salt and pepper, cover and cook slowly on top of the stove for 2-2½ hours. Then cut the breast meat from the pigeons and discard the carcass ; add the aspic to the pan, turn out into a bowl and leave to get cold. Wash and trim the mushrooms, cut in quarters and put in a pie dish with the cooked meats and liquid. Place a pie funnel in the middle of the dish.

Set the oven at 425°F or Mark 7. Roll out the pastry to an oblong just under ¼ inch thick and about 3 inches wider and 4 inches longer than your pie dish. Cut off extra pastry ; roll these trimmings to ⅛ inch thick. From this thinner pastry, cut strips to fit on the rim of the pie dish, and make leaves and a thistle, or rose, from the pastry, for decoration. Dampen the rim of the pie dish and cover with a strip of pastry, pressing it firmly in position, then brush the pastry with cold water. Lift the thicker piece of pastry on your rolling pin and lay it carefully over the top of the pie, taking care not to stretch it. Trim it and press the two layers of pastry on the rim very firmly together ; seal the edges (see page 104).

Add a large pinch of salt to the beaten egg and beat lightly with a fork until the salt dissolves and the egg darkens in colour, this will give the pastry a rich brown and shiny glaze. Brush the top of the pie with the prepared egg wash, decorate suitably with pastry leaves, make a hole in the pastry in the centre of the leaves (above pie funnel) to allow for the escape of steam during cooking time. Brush the decoration with egg wash. Cook the rose or thistle on a baking sheet and put on pie when cooked.

Bake in pre-set hot oven for 20-25 minutes, until pastry is cooked. While the pie is still warm add a little more liquid aspic through hole in centre, if necesary. Serve cold.

Cold beefsteak, pigeon and mushroom pie

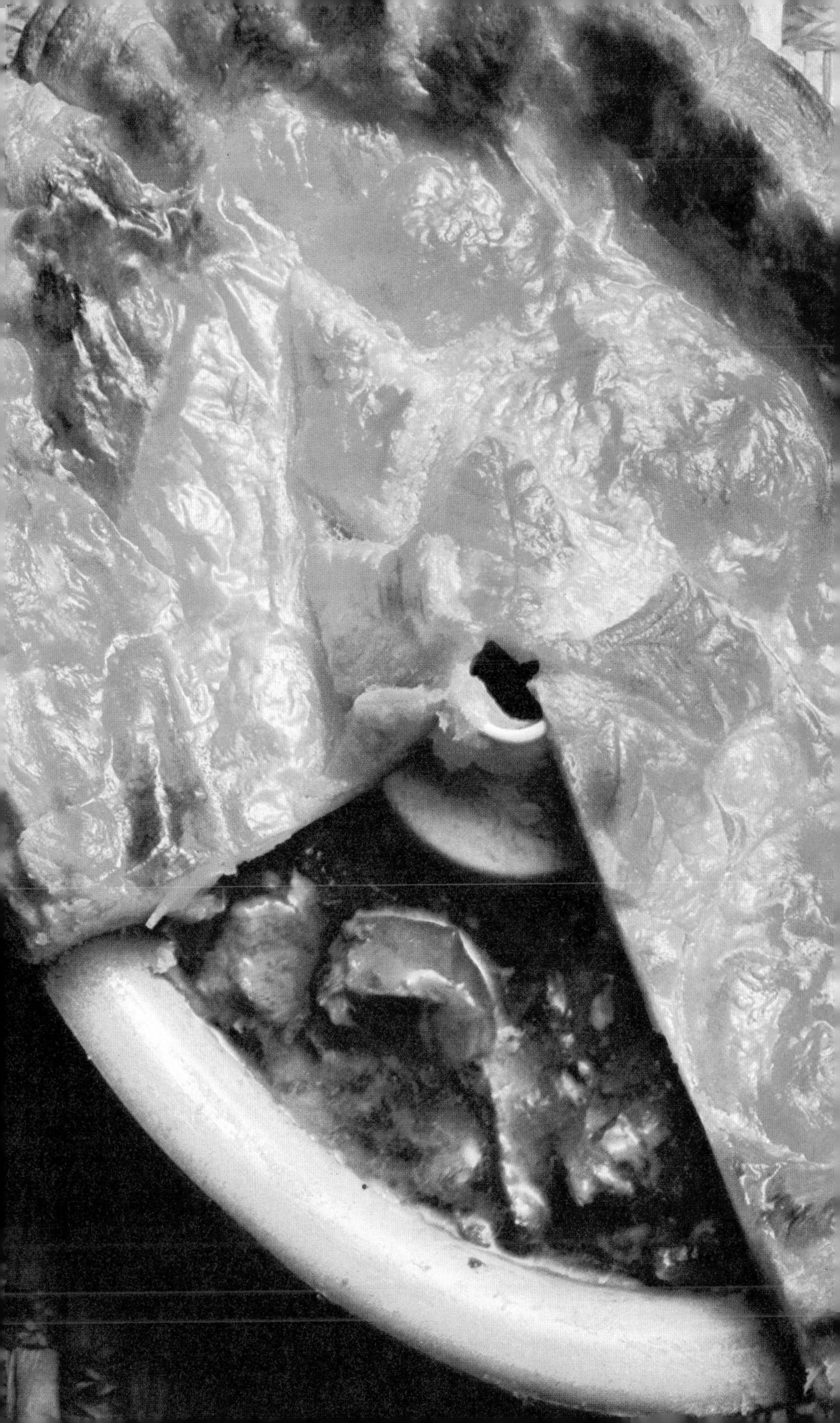

Cornish pasties

For dripping crust pastry
8 oz plain flour
pinch of salt
3 oz good beef dripping
about $2\frac{1}{2}$ fl oz cold water

For filling
8 oz good beefsteak
1 large onion (chopped)
2 medium-size potatoes (finely diced)
1 carrot (finely diced)
$\frac{1}{2}$ small swede, or turnip (finely diced)
salt and pepper

The true Cornish pasty should be made with a good-quality raw steak so that all the flavour and juices of the meat are kept inside the pastry. If properly cooked the meat should not be dry. The vegetables may vary ; for example, some people do not include carrot. The shape is traditional. A pasty should be slightly curved with two blunt horns at each end, rather like a half moon. This quantity makes 4-6 small pasties. Alternatively, 1 large pasty could be made.

Method

Sift the flour with salt, rub in the dripping and mix to a firm dough with the water ; set aside. Set oven at 400°F or Mark 6.

Cut the meat into very small pieces, and mix with prepared vegetables ; season well. Roll out the pastry just over $\frac{1}{4}$ inch thick and cut out into approximately 5-inch squares. Brush round edges with water and put a good tablespoon of the filling mixture on the top edge of each square. Fold over the plain side of the pastry and press the edges together, curving the pastry downwards to form a crescent shape. Crimp edges slightly to seal well.

Bake in pre-set hot oven for 20 minutes. Then cover with wet greaseproof paper (in the case of a large pasty, wrap it round), lower oven to 350°F or Mark 4 and continue to bake for a further 25 30 minutes, when the meat should be well cooked.

1

2

3

1 *For Cornish pasty filling the steak is cut into small pieces, onion is chopped and the rest of the vegetables are finely diced*
2 *The dripping crust pastry is cut into squares, then each square is filled with about 1 tablespoon of the mixture and is folded over*
3 *The cut edges of the pastry are curved downwards to form a crescent shape and they are then crimped slightly to seal*
4 *Cornish pasty, cut open to show the filling of steak, onion, potato, carrot and turnip*

4

Fidget pie

3 gammon rashers
6 oz shortcrust pastry (see page 155)
4-6 medium-size potatoes
3 onions
3 cooking apples
1 tablespoon granulated sugar
salt and pepper
$\frac{1}{2}$ pint, or more, stock (see page 155)
egg wash (egg beaten with a pinch of salt) — optional

8-inch diameter pie dish (about $1\frac{1}{4}$-$1\frac{1}{2}$ pints capacity)

This is a Shropshire dish, a savoury and substantial pie made at harvest time. The essential ingredients are potatoes, onions, apples, bacon or ham.

Method

Set oven at 400°F or Mark 6. Well butter the pie dish. Slice the potatoes thickly, the onions thinly. Peel and quarter the apples then slice them. Remove rind from bacon and cut into strips. Arrange these ingredients in layers in the pie dish, add sugar and season well, then pour over the stock. Cover with the pastry and bake for 30 minutes in the pre-set hot oven. At the end of this time, wrap a double sheet of wet greaseproof paper over and round the pie and continue to bake for a further 30 minutes.

Note : the pie can be gilded and decorated as for a meat pie (see page 96).

Cumberland mutton pies

$\frac{3}{4}$-1 lb slice of mutton (cut from top of leg), or a piece of boned shoulder
8 oz shortcrust pastry (see page 155)
1 medium-size onion (chopped)
1 medium-size carrot (finely diced)
small piece of bayleaf
little salt
black pepper (ground from mill)
egg wash (egg beaten with a pinch of salt)

8-10 large patty pans

The meat for these pies is cut small and kept nicely moist in a well seasoned gravy. They are good eaten hot or cold. The pastry may be hot water crust, flaky — or shortcrust, as suggested here.

Method

Cut the meat into small dice and put into a pan with the vegetables, bayleaf and seasoning. Pour in enough cold water barely to come level with the meat. Set on low heat to simmer until the meat is very tender (about 50 minutes). Draw aside, remove bayleaf and leave until cold.

Set oven at 400°F or Mark 6. Roll out half the pastry, line patty pans and fill them with the meat mixture and a little of the gravy from the meat.

Roll out remaining pastry, stamp it out into rounds and cover the pies. Press down and crimp the edges. Make a little hole in the centre of each. Brush with egg wash and bake in the pre-set hot oven for about 20-30 minutes, or until well browned. Pour in any remaining warmed gravy while the pies are still hot.

Raised pork pie

1 lb pork (lean and fat mixed)
salt and pepper
1 rounded teaspoon mixed dried herbs
$\frac{1}{4}$ pint jellied stock (made from pork bones) — see page 155

For hot water crust
1 lb plain flour
1 teaspoon salt
7 oz lard
$\frac{3}{4}$ pint milk and water (mixed in equal proportions)
milk (for glaze) — optional

1 jar (eg. Kilner jar)

Method

Set oven at 350°F or Mark 4. Dice pork for filling, season well and add herbs.

For hot water crust : warm a mixing bowl and sift in flour and salt, make a well in the centre of the flour.

Heat lard in milk and water. When just boiling, pour into the well in the flour, stir quickly with a wooden spoon until thick, then work with the hand to a dough. Turn on to a board or table, cut off a quarter of the dough, put it back in the warm bowl and cover with a cloth.

Pat out the rest of dough with the fist to a thick round, set a large jar in the centre and work dough up sides. Let dough cool then gently lift out jar.

Watchpoint You must work quickly and mould pastry while it is still warm, otherwise lard sets and pastry becomes brittle.

Fill dough case with meat mixture. Roll or pat out remaining dough to form a lid, leave a small hole in it, then put on top of pie, seal edges. Glaze with milk if wished.

Slide pie on to a baking sheet and bake in pre-set oven for 1-1$\frac{1}{2}$ hours. If pie is getting too brown, cover with damp grease-proof paper towards end of cooking time. Leave till cool before placing a funnel in hole in lid and filling up with jellied stock.

To make a raised pork pie case : work dough up sides of jar while it is still soft enough to handle

Veal and ham pie

8 oz flaky pastry (well chilled) — **see page 156**
1½ lb veal pie meat, or a piece of oyster (shoulder cut)
1 dessertspoon finely chopped onion
1 dessertspoon finely chopped parsley
grated rind of ¼ lemon
4 oz lean cooked ham, or gammon rasher
3 hard-boiled eggs (quartered)
salt and pepper
¾ pint jellied stock (well seasoned) — see page
1 egg (beaten with a pinch of salt)

9-inch long pie dish

Method

Set oven at 425°F or Mark 7. Cut the veal in pieces 1-1½ inches square. Mix chopped onion, parsley and lemon rind together and roll meat in this mixture. Shred the ham, or if a gammon rasher is used, cut off the rind and rust, cut in strips and blanch by putting into boiling water and boiling for ½ minute before draining.

Arrange the meat, ham and quartered eggs in layers till the pie dish is full, doming the top slightly. Pour in stock and three-quarters fill the dish.

Roll out the pastry, cut a strip to cover the edge of the pie dish (slightly dampened),

1

2

3

4

press it down well and then brush with water. Lift the rest of the pastry on to the rolling pin and lay it carefully over the dish. Trim round the edge and seal pastry edges with the back of a knife. This separates the layers so that the pastry puffs up during cooking.

Roll out pastry trimmings and cut leaves for decoration. Make a hole in the centre of the pie with the point of a knife and arrange a decoration around this. The hole will allow steam to escape.

Brush with beaten egg mixed with a large pinch of salt (adding salt to egg gives pastry a very shiny brown glaze). Bake for 1-1$\frac{1}{2}$ hours in pre-set oven.

1 *To cover a veal and ham pie: arrange meat in the pie dish so that it is slightly domed; this will prevent pastry from falling in while cooking. Roll out pastry to shape of dish, then cut off a strip to cover its edge; press down well, then brush with cold water*

2 *Lift rest of pastry on to rolling pin; lay it over pie dish*

3 *Trim edge, seal pastry edge with back of a knife. Make a hole in pie centre to allow steam to escape. Brush the pastry with beaten egg mixture*

4 *Roll out pastry trimmings, cut into leaves, decorate centre and brush leaves with beaten egg*

Rabbit pudding

2 young rabbits
seasoned flour
6 oz salt belly pork
1 rounded tablespoon chopped chives, or fresh herbs
cold water

For suet crust
8 oz self-raising flour
3 oz fresh white breadcrumbs
5 oz shredded suet
salt and pepper
about 4 fl oz cold water (to mix)

6-7 inch diameter pudding basin (1$\frac{1}{2}$ pints capacity)

Imported boned rabbit is now available in Britain and is ideal for this recipe; use about 1 lb.

Method

Grease the pudding basin. Joint the rabbits, cutting the legs in half and the back into 3 or 4 pieces. Trim away any flaps of skin, excess bone and the wings (forelegs). Soak the trimmed joints overnight in salted water. Then drain, rinse and dry thoroughly, and roll in seasoned flour. Cut the pork into cubes, removing any bone, then blanch and drain.

To prepare suet crust: mix dry ingredients together, then add the water to make a soft dough. Roll two-thirds of the dough and line the greased pudding basin with it. Pack the pieces of rabbit and pork into the basin, adding the herbs, and pour in about $\frac{1}{4}$ pint water. Roll out the remaining piece of pastry and cover the top; press well down around the edge. Cover with foil and steam for 3 hours.

Serve pudding in the basin with a napkin tied round.

Rabbit pie

2 young rabbits
8 oz flaky pastry (see page 154)
stock, or water (see method)
seasoned flour
½ lb streaky bacon rashers
1 medium-size onion (finely chopped)
2 tablespoons chopped mixed herbs
grated rind of ½ lemon
salt and pepper
pinch of ground mace
beaten egg (for glazing)

8-9 inch long pie dish (1½ pints capacity)

Method

Joint the rabbits and soak overnight in salted water. Use the wings and rib cage to make some strong well-flavoured stock (by simmering bones with vegetables and herbs to flavour for 1-2 hours); then strain and cool.

Set oven at 400°F or Mark 6.

Drain, rinse and dry the rabbit joints, trimming away any skin etc. Roll the joints in the flour. Cut the bacon rashers into strips crosswise (lardons) and mix with the onion, herbs, lemon rind and seasonings. Pack the rabbit into the pie dish, layering it with the bacon mixture. Pour in enough stock to come two-thirds up the side of the pie dish.

Watchpoint For pies of this sort, made with raw ingredients, watch that the contents do not come above the level of the edge of the pie dish, otherwise they cannot cook properly.

Roll out the pastry, cover dish as for a steak and kidney pie, glaze and decorate (see page 92).

Bake in pre-set hot oven for 30-35 minutes or until the pastry is risen and well browned. Then wrap pie in a double sheet of wet greaseproof paper. Lower heat to 325°F or Mark 3 and continue to bake for a further hour.

Sealing pastry edges

Lightly flour the back of your forefinger, hold it firmly on pastry rim and, using the back of a knife, flick-cut the pastry edge all round. The pressure from your finger is sufficient to seal pastry together and cutting with the back of the knife helps the pastry to rise and have an attractive flaky appearance.

Boiling, steaming and pot roasting

Boiling

Boiling is the most simple and economical form of cooking. The word implies that the food is immersed and cooked in water and, for better or worse, has become known internationally as the English way of cooking. (You will always find plainly boiled potatoes described on a continental menu as Pommes à l'anglaise.)

Meat can be boiled in two different ways :

1 A joint such as leg of mutton is plunged into boiling salted water and boiled for 5 minutes to firm the outside and so seal in the juices. The heat is then reduced and the meat simmered until tender. Place the meat in the pan with the side that is to be uppermost when dished up on the bottom. Skim frequently during cooking time and allow 20-25 minutes per pound and 20-25 minutes over.

2 Meat for soups, stocks and beef tea is covered with cold water, salt added, and then allowed to stand for up to 20 minutes before cooking. This is because cold water and salt draw out the juices of the meat. Length of cooking time depends on the weight of meat and only gentle heat should be applied. To get as much flavour into liquid as possible, cut meat into small pieces.

Note : Salted meats — beef, ham, pork and tongue — should be put into tepid water to prevent over-saltiness.

Bacon joints for boiling

Various parts of the baconer are used as joints for boiling. Gammon joints, which are taken from the hind leg, are best, and are usually cooked and served as ham.

Gammon differs from prepared ham : for the latter the thigh is removed from the untreated side of bacon and cured separately. Ham is rounded, not cut squarely from the carcass like gammon. The weight of a gammon varies from 12-16 lb and can be divided into the following four joints :

Corner gammon. The average weight is 4-4$\frac{1}{2}$ lb. A good, lean joint with a nice rim of fat ; it is best boiled and can be served hot or cold. Gammon rashers are cut from this joint.

Middle gammon. The average weight is 5-6 lb. Like corner, but can be divided into joints of 1$\frac{1}{2}$-2 lb, so it is convenient for a small family. Boil it and serve hot or cold.

Gammon hock. The average weight is 5-6 lb. This joint is especially suitable for partially cooking by boiling, then baking, well sprinkled with brown sugar and basted with cider. Compared with other gammon joints hock has less cut surface and more outside fat, so the flesh is less inclined to dry.

Gammon rashers are cut from this joint.

Gammon slipper. The average weight is 1$\frac{1}{2}$ lb. Suitable for a small family for one meal. Boil it and serve it hot or cold.

Cooking a bacon joint

All joints benefit from being soaked in cold water before cooking to remove excess salt. The time varies between 2 and 24 hours according to the size of the joint and whether it is smoked or unsmoked.

All joints are best cooked with root vegetables in the water to flavour — in some country districts a wisp of hay is added.

With large joints use the back of a knife to scrape the rind and underside to remove any 'rust'.

Most small joints are sold boned, but whole gammon and hams are not.

Skinning joints

All boiling joints should be skinned before serving. If serving cold first allow the joint to cool in the liquid, then lift it out and peel off the skin. Coat the skinned fat with raspings (browned crumbs). If serving hot, skin in the same way and use joint according to recipe.

The ease with which the skin can be peeled off is a test of how cooked the bacon is.

Cooking times

Small joints

1 lb and under : 45 minutes
1$\frac{1}{2}$-2 lb : 1-1$\frac{1}{2}$ hours
3 lb and over : 30 minutes per lb

Gammon and hams

Allow 20 minutes per lb and 20 minutes over

Steaming

Steaming is cooking by moist heat, a comparatively slow method as the food does not come into direct contact with boiling water but only with its vapour. Steaming food takes half as long again as boiling, and twice as long if the texture of the food is particularly dense.

There are two ways of steaming :
1 Using a steamer — a container with perforations at the bottom and a close-fitting lid. This can be bought with graduated ridges at the base rim so that it will fit snugly on to saucepans of varying sizes. For a perfect fit, saucepans can be bought complete with matching steamers. The food is placed directly in the top half — the steamer — and therefore comes in immediate contact with the steam. This method is used for vegetables such as potatoes ; puddings ; fish and poultry. Different foods wrapped separately in parchment paper can be cooked together in one steamer.
2 Using two plates. The food to be cooked is put between two plates over a pan of boiling water and cooks in its own juice and steam. The result is delicate in flavour and easily digested — an ideal way of cooking for invalids.

Two methods of steaming. Left, steaming chops between two plates over a saucepan of boiling water makes the meat more easily digested. Right, using a saucepan with a matching steamer for vegetables, puddings, fish or poultry

Pot roasting

Pot roasting is one of the best and easiest ways of dealing with the cheaper cuts of meat that need slow cooking to prevent them from becoming dry and tasteless. Poultry is also excellent pot roasted, not only the older boiling fowls, but roasting birds and baby chickens too, because they keep all their flavour and succulence.

This method has the great advantage of requiring the minimum of attention once the meat is cooking. The only proviso is that you must have the right type of pot or casserole. This should be of thick iron, enamelled iron or aluminium with a close-fitting lid, deep and big enough to hold a joint or bird comfortably.

The procedure is simple: meat or bird is browned all over, root vegetables and a bouquet garni are added, but no liquid unless stipulated in the recipe. Even then it should not be more than one-eighth of a pint, ie. a small wineglass of stock or wine. A small quantity of seasoning is also added. Close the lid tightly and set on a low heat; if more convenient, put into a slow oven. Cooking time depends on the size of joint or bird, and is indicated in specific recipes.

Meat is served as for a roast, with vegetables cooked separately. If vegetables were cooked with the meat, they would have little flavour and would be overcooked. The flavour will be in the gravy; this is strained off, well skimmed of fat and may be diluted with a little stock.

Once pot roasted, meat or chicken can be served in different ways, varied by sauces and garnishes.

Beef 'en daube'

3-4 lb piece of aitchbone, or topside of beef
1 pigs trotter
pepper (ground from mill)
½ pint stock (see page 155), or water
6-8 oz salted belly pork
¾ lb ripe tomatoes (skinned, seeds removed, flesh chopped)
8 green olives (stoned and sliced)

For marinade
2-3 tablespoons olive oil
1 dessertspoon wine vinegar
½ bottle red wine
1 onion (sliced)
1 carrot (sliced)
1 large bouquet garni (including bayleaf, thyme, parsley stalks and a strip of orange rind)
6 peppercorns
1 clove
½ dozen coriander seeds, or ½ teaspoon ground coriander

This is a dish where the meat is first marinated and then cooked very slowly until tender. There are several variations of a daube but the essential is the long, slow, even cooking. Remember that a daube should be so tender that a spoon — not a knife — is used to cut the meat.

Method

Put all the ingredients for the marinade into a pan, bring slowly to the boil, then draw aside and allow to get quite cold. Place beef in a deep dish and pour over the marinade. Leave for 2-3 days (in warm weather keep meat covered in the refrigerator) turning it over several times.

Then take out the meat and strain the marinade, reserving the vegetables, herbs and spices. Skim the oil from the surface of the marinade and put this into a thick iron or aluminium casserole large enough to hold the beef comfortably; heat, and when the oil is hot, brown the meat and pigs trotter all over. Draw aside, add the marinade, and the reserved bouquet garni, vegetables, and the spices tied in a piece of muslin. Season with pepper only, and add the stock. Bring slowly to boil, cover and put in to slow oven, at 275°F or Mark 1. Leave about 7-8 hours, when the daube should be very tender.

Meanwhile simmer the pork in water for 30-40 minutes, then take up and cut into lardons. Add these to the daube after the first 2 hours' cooking. Add the tomatoes to the daube 1 hour before the end of cooking time.

To dish up, take out the trotter, fork the meat off the bone and cut into shreds, return to the casserole with the olives, first taking out the bouquet garni. Set beef on serving dish, leave whole or slice as much as required. Reboil the gravy, skim and spoon some over the dish and serve the rest separately.

Beef pot roast

$2\frac{1}{2}$ lb joint topside beef
1 tablespoon dripping
1 onion (stuck with a clove)
1 carrot (sliced)
bouquet garni
salt
pepper (ground from mill)
1 wineglass red wine, or stock (see page 155)
1 dessertspoon plain flour (for gravy)
little extra stock, or water, to taste

Method

Heat dripping in the pot. Put the meat in and brown well on all sides. Take out and pour off any surplus fat, leaving 1 tablespoon on the bottom. Replace meat and tuck the prepared vegetables down the sides with the herbs.

Pour over liquid and season very lightly. Lay a piece of buttered paper over the meat so that the cover fits tightly on top and there is no danger of the meat getting hard from contact with the lid while cooking. Set on low heat or, if preferred, in the oven at 325°F or Mark 3. Cook at least 2-3 hours or until the meat is tender, turning it over once or twice if cooking on the top of the stove.

Dish up the meat, skim off the fat, strain off the juice. Mix 1 dessertspoon of this fat with 1 dessertspoon flour. Add to the juice and dilute with a little extra stock or water to taste, and boil for about 5 minutes to cook the flour. This meat juice is concentrated.

Slice meat for serving, spoon over gravy. Garnish with vegetables or serve them separately.

Boiled beef and dumplings

4-5 lb salted silverside of beef
3-4 onions (peeled)
3-4 carrots (peeled and quartered)
1 small cabbage (quartered)
pepper

For dumplings
8 oz self-raising flour
5 oz suet (chopped, or shredded)
$\frac{1}{2}$ teaspoon salt
about $\frac{3}{4}$ cup of cold water

The beef should be cooked for 25-30 minutes per lb, so plan the time accordingly. Put in the dumplings 20-30 minutes before end of this cooking time.

Method

Place beef in a large pan, cover completely with cold water and bring slowly to the boil.

Watchpoint Keep liquid well skimmed of fat when coming to the boil. A dash or two of cold water will help to bring the scum to the surface. This, coupled with gentle simmering, will keep the liquor clear (especially important if it is also to be used for soup).

Cover pan and simmer beef for about 50 minutes. Then add the onions and the carrots. Cook gently for a further 15 minutes before adding the cabbage. Then leave the meat cooking while making dumplings.

To prepare dumplings: mix the flour, suet and salt together. Add enough water to make a fairly firm dough. Divide this into walnut-size pieces. Roll lightly in a little flour and drop into the pan with the beef, so that they simmer during the final 20-30 minutes of cooking time. Keep the pan covered and turn the dumplings once during this time.

Watchpoint When adding the dumplings make sure they have plenty of room to swell. If the pan is very full, it is better to cook them separately.

Taste, add pepper if necessary.

To serve, take out the dump lings with a draining spoon and arrange round a large dish with the vegetables. Set the beef in the centre and serve some of the liquor in a sauce boat.

Pot roast leg of lamb

with spring vegetables

$3\frac{1}{2}$-4 lb leg of lamb
2 oz butter
$\frac{1}{2}$ clove of garlic (crushed with $\frac{1}{2}$ teaspoon salt) — optional
1 tablespoon chopped parsley
1 wineglass white wine
1 wineglass jellied stock (see page 155)
salt
black pepper (ground from mill)
1 lb new potatoes
$\frac{3}{4}$ lb baby carrots
$\frac{1}{2}$ lb shelled broad beens
1 small packet of frozen petits pois
1 teaspoon granulated sugar
1 tablespoon plain flour
1 small carton (about $2\frac{1}{2}$ fl oz) single cream

Method

Remove the shank bone from the leg of lamb and use to make the jellied stock. Cut away the fine skin and any fat that is cover ing the joint.

Soften the butter in a bowl with a wooden spoon, work in the crushed garlic and the parsley ; spread this butter over the lamb and leave it for about 15 minutes. Then put the pre pared joint in a large, heavy flameproof casserole, cover and set over a gentle heat for about 30 minutes. Shake the pan occasionally during this period to prevent the lamb from sticking ; at the end of this time the lamb should have changed colour (from pink to grey) but it should not be brown.

Set oven at 375°F or Mark 5. Now pour the wine into the casserole and leave it bubbling gently until it has reduced by about one-third, then pour on the stock and season. Cover the pan and put in the pre-set oven for about 1-$1\frac{1}{2}$ hours.

Watchpoint Look at the joint after the first 30 minutes ; if your casserole is of enamelled iron (as opposed to earthenware), you will probably need to lower the heat of the oven to 325°F or Mark 3. The meat should cook gently.

Prepare the fresh vegetables and add to casserole 1 hour before the end of cooking time. Strain the gravy from casserole but do not remove the meat. Add frozen petits pois and sugar, cover casserole and return to the oven. Turn the oven to its lowest setting while preparing the sauce.

To prepare sauce ; skim fat from the cooking liquor, mix with the flour and return to the liquid. Tip this into a small pan and stir until boiling ; then simmer for 2-3 minutes. Add the cream and reheat ; taste the sauce for seasoning.

Dish up the meat, surround with vegetables (enough to make it look pretty but not to get in the way of the carver) and spoon over a little sauce. Pour the rest of the sauce over the vegetables, which should be served in a deep dish.

Above : fresh and frozen vegetables for garnish are left in the pan with the meat after gravy has been strained off for sauce

Below : finished pot roast leg of lamb

Pot roast shoulder of lamb

1 shoulder of lamb (boned)
2 medium-size onions (sliced)
1 tablespoon dripping
1-2 sticks of celery, or ½ turnip (sliced)
2 carrots (sliced)
1 oz kneaded butter (see page 28), or little arrowroot (mixed with water)

For stuffing
8 oz pork sausage meat
1 medium-size onion (finely chopped)
1 tablespoon dripping
1-2 parsley stalks
1 tablespoon mixed chopped herbs
1 clove of garlic (optional)
salt and pepper

Trussing needle and string or poulty pins / lacers

Method

Bone out the lamb or get the butcher to do it for you. Prepare the stuffing : heat 1 tablespoon of dripping in pan, add chopped onion and cook until soft.

Then add to the sausage meat with herbs, crushed garlic, if used, and seasoning. Put stuffing into lamb ; sew up or fasten with poultry pins. Brown the meat in hot dripping in the pot. Take out meat and put in sliced root vegetables. Allow them to colour, then drain off any surplus fat. Replace shoulder of lamb and cover the pot tightly.

Cook slowly for 1½ hours on top of stove or in the oven at 300°F or Mark 2. Then take up meat, remove string or pins, strain off liquid and skim well. Add a little extra stock, if necessary, and thicken lightly with kneaded butter, or a little arrowroot. Serve vegetables separately with this pot roast.

Ham Veronique

1 corner gammon, or cut of middle gammon
few root vegetables (sliced) — for flavouring
bouquet garni
½ lb green grapes
lemon juice

For sauce
1 wineglass dry white wine
1 dessertspoon finely chopped onion
2 egg yolks
3 oz butter

For sauce
1 oz butter
1 rounded tablespoon plain flour
½-¾ pint veal stock (see page 156)
2½ fl oz single cream, or top of milk

Method

Cover the gammon with water and simmer with the sliced vegetables and bouquet garni, allowing 20 minutes per lb and 20 minutes over. Cool a little in the liquid.

Peel and pip the grapes, add a few drops of lemon juice and keep covered in a bowl.

To prepare sauce : boil the wine with the onion to reduce by about a third. Cream egg yolks well, then strain on the wine, add a good nut of the butter and work the mixture in a bain-marie (or double saucepan) until thick. Then add the rest of the butter, a little at a time, until the sauce has the consistency of thick cream, but do not boil. Set aside.

To prepare the roux : melt 1 oz butter in a pan, add flour, cook for 1 minute; then pour on the stock. Blend and stir until boiling. Cook for a few minutes. Draw pan aside, beat in butter sauce, add cream or milk and reheat slowly. Do not allow to boil. Add the grapes and set aside.

Take up the ham, remove skin, slice and arrange in a dish. Coat with a little of the sauce and serve the rest separately. The dish may be garnished with new potatoes.

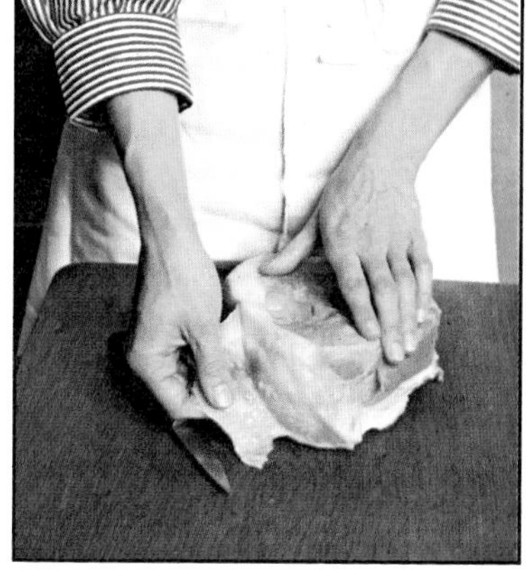

Right : when ham is cooked and has cooled a little the skin should be peeled off carefully

Raw ingredients for ham Véronique, which is first simmered with root vegetables. The name 'Véronique' denotes the use of grapes in the sauce

Hot boiled gammon

2 lb middle cut of gammon
8 even-size carrots
4 even-size onions
6 peppercorns
1 bayleaf

By cooking whole onions and carrots in with the ham and serving them arranged round the joint, you will need only one other vegetable and we suggest potatoes in white sauce (see right).

Method

Cover the joint with cold water, bring it slowly to the boil and then skim well. Add onions, carrots and seasonings, cover and simmer for 1-1½ hours (that is about 20 minutes per lb and 20 minutes over). Leave the gammon to stand in the liquid at least 15 minutes before skinning and carving. (The liquid can be kept and used for soup.)

Drain the vegetables and arrange them around carved gammon on the serving dish.

Potatoes in white sauce

1 lb new potatoes
parsley (chopped)

For white sauce
1½ oz butter
1¼ oz plain flour
¾ pint milk
salt and pepper

Method

Scrape potatoes and put into boiling salted water ; cover pan and boil for 20-30 minutes, or until tender. Drain, place over gentle heat for a few minutes to dry. Prepare white sauce by first making a roux, blending in the milk and seasoning. Drain the potatoes, add them to the sauce and heat carefully without boiling ; then add the parsley and serve. Add the chopped parsley just before turning the potatoes into the serving dish.
Note : when new potatoes are not available use canned ones. These are delicious served in a white sauce.

Boiled gammon is served with whole carrots and onions, and new potatoes in white sauce

Ham à la crème

2 lb middle cut of gammon
1 onion (stuck with a clove)
6 peppercorns
1 bayleaf
½ oz butter

For cream sauce
1½ oz butter
1½ tablespoons plain flour
1 wineglass stock (see page 156)
½ pint milk
salt
black pepper (ground from mill)
5 tablespoons single cream, or top of milk
2 tablespoons finely grated Gruyère, or Parmesan, cheese

Method

Cover the joint with cold water, bring slowly to the boil and then skim well. Add the onion and seasonings, cover and simmer for 1-1½ hours. Leave the gammon to stand in the liquid at least 15 minutes before removing the skin and carving.

To prepare the sauce: melt the butter, stir in the flour and then blend in the stock and milk. Season with a little salt and plenty of black pepper. Simmer the sauce gently for 15 minutes, then add the cream or milk. Stir well, add the cheese and adjust the seasoning.

Pour a little of the cream sauce into an ovenproof dish, carve the ham into even slices and arrange on top. Spoon over the rest of the sauce, then cover with ½ oz butter in shavings.

Brown ham in a hot oven at 400°F or Mark 6 for 5-10 minutes, or glaze under grill.

Lamb pot roast

4½ lb leg of lamb
2 tablespoons salad oil
salt and pepper
a little cornflour

Method

Heat the salad oil in a large heavy pan. Put in the leg of lamb and cook gently, turning until all sides are nicely coloured. This should take about 30 minutes. Season lightly, put in 2 tablespoons of water, cover tightly and cook very gently for 1¾-2 hours.

For serving take up the lamb, tip ½ pint of hot water into the pan and boil up well. Season to taste and thicken the gravy with a little cornflour mixed to a paste with water. Serve with vegetables separately.

Braising

Cheaper cuts of meat are often full of flavour but inclined to be tough, so braising is the ideal way of cooking them. The meat is tender and succulent and the rich, strong gravy it was cooked in is a bonus. For a good braise it's essential to use a very small quantity of liquid in a pot with a tight-fitting lid. The meat cooks in the steam from the liquid, thus keeping moist. Most of the cooking is done in the oven so that the braise has both top and bottom heat.

Choosing the right pan is important ; it should be of enamelled iron, cast iron or thick aluminium and be deep enough for the joint to fit snugly into it. Glass, or any non-flameproof ovenware, however, is not suitable as part of the cooking is done on top of the stove.

Braising meat

Heat the pan and add 2 tablespoons of oil or dripping. When hot, put in the meat and brown well all over. Take out meat and put in a good plateful of sliced or diced vegetables (onion, carrot, a little turnip and celery). This is called a mirepoix.

Cover pan and cook gently (or sweat) for 5-7 minutes. This allows the juice to run from the vegetables and lets them absorb excess fat. Put back the meat on top of the mirepoix, together with a bouquet garni and a little seasoning.

Pour in liquid as required in the recipe. This should cover the bottom of the pan up to a level of 2-3 inches. Cover closely and cook for 1-2 hours (according to the size of the joint) in a slow oven at 325°F or Mark 3.

Baste and turn the meat occasionally ; it should be very tender when cooked. If you choose to braise a roasting joint, less time can be allowed (20 minutes per lb and 20 minutes over).

When meat is tender, remove it from pan and keep warm. Strain the gravy and skim surface well to take off any fat. A sauce can be added, depending on the recipe, or gravy can be thickened with kneaded butter or arrowroot. The vegetables

cooked with the braise are now discarded ; they have done their job of flavouring and will be overcooked.

When braising a roasting joint, such as a leg of lamb, the vegetables can be served with the meat as the cooking time is not so long.

Watchpoint For a really successful braise it is essential to have a slightly jellied brown stock (see page 157). If the stock is not strong, a pig's foot (trotter) tucked in beside the joint gives a beautifully 'sticky' texture to the finished sauce.

Braising vegetables

Good braising vegetables are onions, celery, chicory, cabbage and lettuce. They are first blanched (for root vegetables, put into cold water and bring to the boil ; for green vegetables, put into boiling water and reboil before draining thoroughly). This blanching is done to remove any strong flavour, and to soften the outside and so ensure thorough cooking.

Joints for braising

Beef	Aitchbone, topside, top rump, top rib, brisket.
Mutton or Lamb	Leg, shoulder (plain, or boned and stuffed), loin (boned and stuffed).
Veal	Cuts from leg and shoulder (plain, or boned and stuffed).

Braised brisket

3 lb piece brisket of beef

For braising
1-2 tablespoons beef dripping, or salad oil
2 onions
2 carrots
2 sticks of celery
salt and pepper
bouquet garni
$\frac{1}{4}$ pint stock (see page 155)

For sauce
1-2 tablespoons dripping, or oil
1 tablespoon plain flour
$\frac{3}{4}$ pint stock
1 teaspoon tomato purée

Brisket has slightly more fat than most joints, but it makes a succulent dish. If you prefer leaner meat, take a cut from the aitchbone or topside.

Method

Set the oven at 325°F or Mark 3. Heat the braising pan and put in 1-2 tablespoons dripping or oil. When hot, put in the meat and brown on all sides. Take out meat and lower the heat. Have ready the vegetables, sliced or diced, add them to the pan, cover and cook gently for 5-7 minutes.

Then set the joint on top, season, add bouquet garni and pour round stock. Cover and cook in pre-set oven for $1\frac{1}{2}$-2 hours, or until very tender.

Meanwhile prepare the sauce. Melt dripping in a saucepan, stir in the flour. If this roux is too stiff, add more dripping to make it spread nicely over the bottom of the pan. Cook slowly to a russet-brown, then draw aside, cool and pour on the stock. Blend, then add tomato purée ; simmer uncovered for 15-20 minutes.

When meat is tender, remove from dish and slice what is needed. The remaining meat can be lightly pressed between two heavy plates (this makes meat easier to cut) and eaten cold. Dish up the sliced meat, cover and keep hot.

Strain gravy and skim well with a spoon to remove fat. Add gravy to the sauce, boil well until thick and syrupy. Spoon enough over the meat to moisten it and serve hot with creamed potatoes and parsnips or swedes.

Braised beef provençale

2½ lb aitchbone, or topside, of beef
2 large tablespoons olive, or salad, oil
1 large carrot
1 large onion
1 clove of garlic (peeled)
6 peppercorns
bouquet garni
1 wineglass red wine
¼ pint good stock (see page 155)
salt and pepper

For sauce
1 tablespoon oil
1 tablespoon plain flour
½ pint jellied stock (see page 155)

For garnish
4 ripe tomatoes
6-8 green olives

Method

Set the oven at 325°F or Mark 3. Brown the beef in oil in the braising pan, then remove. Dice or slice carrot and onion, add to pan and lower the heat. Cook slowly, uncovered, to allow the vegetables to colour a little but keep moist. Put the meat on vegetables, add garlic (whole), peppercorns, bouquet garni, wine and stock. Season lightly, cover tightly and braise for about 2 hours, or until tender, in pre-set oven. Turn and baste meat occasionally.

Meanwhile prepare sauce. Heat oil, stir in flour and cook gently. When a rich brown, stir in the stock, bring to the boil and boil gently for 7-10 minutes.

Remove cooked meat from pan, strain off gravy, skim well to remove fat, then add gravy to sauce. Boil until thick and syrupy, and well flavoured. Remove from heat.

To prepare garnish : scald and skin tomatoes, cut in quarters, flick out the seeds and cut away the small piece of stalk on each quarter. Add tomatoes to the sauce with the olives, cut in spirals or quarters to remove stones. Slice meat and keep hot in dish.

Bring sauce to the boil again and spoon over the meat. Serve hot with creamed potatoes, or braised chicory.

Watchpoint Bring the sauce quickly to the boil once olives and tomatoes have been added. Any cooking of the olives would make the sauce too salty.

Braised beef with red wine

$2\frac{1}{2}$-3 lb joint topside, or aitchbone, of beef
marinade for beef (see right)
1 onion
1 carrot
2 tablespoons oil, or dripping
bouquet garni
1 clove of garlic
salt and pepper
1 wineglass Burgundy
1 wineglass good stock (see page 155

For sauce
1 tablespoon oil
1 tablespoon plain flour
$\frac{1}{2}$ pint stock
1 teaspoon tomato purée
6 oz button mushrooms

For garnish
8 oz button onions (glazed with $\frac{1}{2}$ oz butter and 1 teaspoon granulated sugar)

Method

Prepare the marinade and leave meat standing in it in a cool place for 24 hours.

To cook, take the meat from the marinade and dab it dry with absorbent paper. Slice the onion and carrot. Heat a deep braising pan, put in the dripping or oil and brown the meat all over. Take out meat and add the vegetables, lower heat and fry gently until coloured. Put back the meat, add the bouquet garni, garlic (whole or crushed with salt) and seasoning. Pour in the wine and stock. Cover the pan and braise gently for about 2-2$\frac{1}{2}$ hours or until tender in oven pre-set at 325°F or Mark 3.

Meanwhile prepare the sauce. Heat oil, stir in flour and brown slowly and well. Draw pan aside, add the stock and tomato purée, and strain in the marinade. Bring to the boil and simmer 15-20 minutes, skim surface of sauce occasionally with a tablespoon to remove fat. Wash mushrooms, trim the stalks level with the caps but do not peel. Add mushrooms to sauce and continue to simmer for 3-4 minutes.

To prepare garnish ; peel the onions, blanch and put in a pan with butter and sugar. Cover tightly and cook gently, shaking pan occasionally. In 6-7 minutes the onions will be glazed.

Remove cooked beef from pan, slice as much as required and keep hot. Boil gravy to reduce a little and strain into the sauce. Spoon enough over the beef to moisten it nicely and serve the rest separately. Garnish dish with glazed onions. Serve leftover meat cold.

Marinade for beef

(for a joint of about 2$\frac{1}{2}$ lb)

1 large onion
1 large carrot
1 stick of celery (optional)
1 large clove of garlic (peeled)
6-8 peppercorns
2 tablespoons olive oil
bouquet garni
2 wineglasses red wine (Burgundy or Burgundy-type, or any robust red wine)

Method

Cut the vegetables into thin slices, bruise the peeled clove of garlic but leave whole (chop garlic if a stronger flavour is liked). Put these into a pan with the other ingredients, cover and bring to the boil. Simmer for 2 minutes, then pour off and leave until cold.

Armenian lamb with pilaf

2 lb fillet end of leg of lamb
1 tablespoon oil
1 oz butter
2 medium-size onions (sliced)
1 clove of garlic (chopped)
1 tablespoon plain flour
1 teaspoon ground cumin seed
½ teaspoon ground allspice
2 tablespoons tomato purée
½-¾ pint stock (see page 155)
salt and pepper

Method

Cut the meat from the bone and divide into 2-inch squares. Heat the oil in a sauté pan or flameproof casserole, drop in the butter and, when foaming, brown the meat a few pieces at a time.

Remove the meat, add the onions and garlic and cook slowly for 5 minutes, stirring from time to time; dust in the flour and spices and continue cooking a further 3-4 minutes. Stir in the tomato purée and ½ pint of stock, away from the heat, and blend until mixture is smooth.

Return pan to the stove and stir mixture until boiling; reduce the heat, add the meat to pan, cover and cook for 45-60 minutes on top of the stove or in the oven at 350°F or Mark 4. Stir the mixture occasionally, adding the reserved stock, if necessary, and season to taste.

Dish up the meat on a serving dish, piling it up neatly. Reduce the gravy to a thick sauce, if necessary, and spoon it over. There should be sufficient to moisten it. Arrange pilaf (see opposite page) at each end of the dish or serve it separately. Serve a green salad in season.

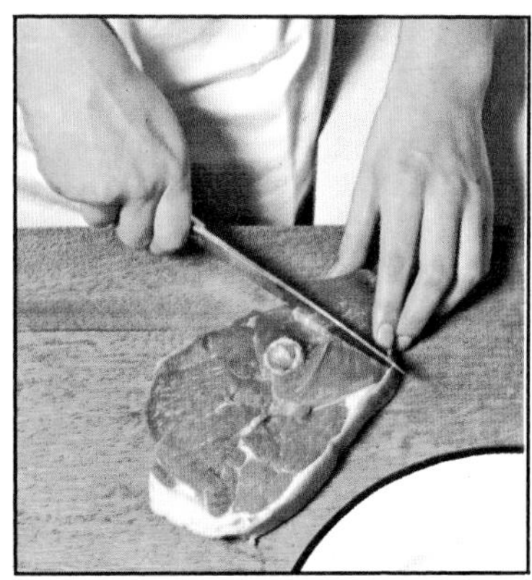

Prepare the meat for Armenian lamb by removing the bone from the fillet end of leg of lamb and cutting the meat into two-inch squares ready for browning

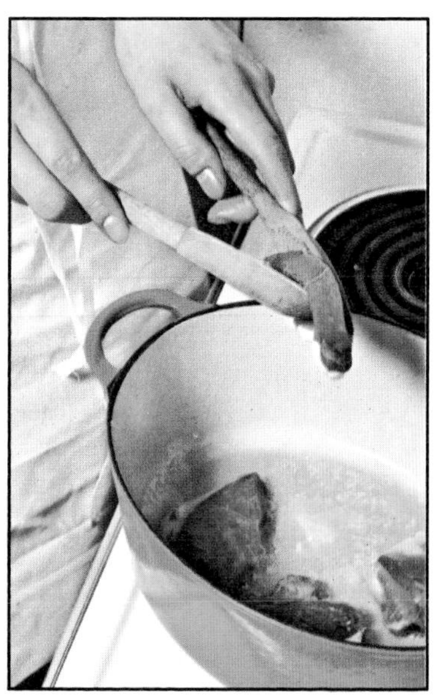

Heat the oil in a sauté pan or deep casserole and add the butter. When the butter is foaming, drop in a few pieces of lamb at a time and cook each piece and brown on all sides

Pilaf

1½ oz butter
1 small onion (finely chopped)
8½ oz long grain rice
¾ pint chicken stock (see page 155)
salt and pepper
3 oz currants (washed)
3 oz pistachio nuts

Method

To blanch pistachios, pour boiling water over, add a pinch of bicarbonate of soda to preserve the colour. Cover and leave to cool. Drain, rinse and press skins off with fingers. Then split the nuts in half.

Melt two-thirds of the butter in a flameproof casserole, add the onion and cook slowly until just golden-brown ; stir in the rice and continue cooking for 2-3 minutes. Pour on the stock, season and bring it to the boil. Cover the casserole and cook in the oven at 375°F or Mark 5 until the rice is tender (about 20 minutes).

Add extra stock to moisten, if necessary, and put the rest of the butter in casserole, with the currants and pistachio nuts, forking them in very carefully.

Breast of lamb Fallette

2 small lean breasts of lamb (about 2 lb in all)
1 large onion
2 carrots
2 sticks of celery
3-4 bacon rashers
bouquet garni
½ pint jellied bone stock (see page 155)
chopped parsley

For stuffing
2 lambs kidneys
6 oz cooked ham (shoulder cut)
½ clove of garlic
2 oz fresh white breadcrumbs
1 large handful of spinach leaves (about 5 oz)
1 small egg (beaten)
salt and pepper

For brown sauce
2 shallots
1 oz butter
¾ oz plain flour
1 rounded teaspoon tomato purée
¾ pint brown stock
bouquet garni

Method

Bone out the breasts of lamb and split them carefully at the side to form a pocket in each one.

Set oven at 350°F or Mark 4.

Dice the braising vegetables, line the bottom of a deep flameproof pan or casserole with the bacon rashers and place the vegetables on these. Cover pan and set it on a low heat to sweat the vegetables.

To prepare stuffing : skin and core kidneys and chop with the ham and garlic. Stir in the breadcrumbs, then finely chop the spinach and add with the egg to the mixture. Season well. Fill stuffing into the pockets in the breasts, taking care not to stuff them too tightly, then sew up with fine string.

Set breasts on the braising vegetables, add bouquet garni and pour around the stock. Put lamb to cook (uncovered) in preset moderate oven for about 1-1½ hours, basting it occasionally.

Meanwhile prepare brown sauce : chop the shallots finely and soften them in half the butter ; add the remaining butter, blend in the flour and allow it to brown slowly. Draw pan aside, add tomato purée and stock. Bring sauce to boil, add bouquet garni, season lightly and simmer, uncovered, for 20-25 minutes, skimming it if necessary. Then strain sauce.

When the meat is tender and brown, lift out of pan or casserole, remove the string and dish up. Coat it with a little of the sauce and dust thickly with chopped parsley. Serve the rest of the sauce in a sauce boat, and accompany with creamed potatoes, and cabbage.

Top left : splitting the breasts at the sides to form pockets
Top right : sewing up breasts with string and a trussing needle
Below right : the finished dish

Braised veal Orloff

2½ lb fillet of veal
1 oz butter
1 large onion (diced)
2 carrots (diced)
1 stick of celery (diced)
1 wineglass white wine
½ pint stock **(see page 155)**
salt and pepper
bouquet garni
1 rounded teaspoon arrowroot (mixed with 1 tablespoon cold water)

For soubise
2 large onions (chopped)
½ oz butter
3 oz Carolina rice
¼ pint stock
salt and pepper
1 egg yolk
1 tablespoon cream

For mornay sauce
1 oz butter
1 rounded tablespoon plain flour
½ pint milk
2-3 tablespoons grated cheese
1 tablespoon cream

To garnish
8 oz mushrooms
¼ oz butter
salt and pepper
squeeze of lemon juice

Method

Set oven at 350°F or Mark 4.

Tie the veal neatly with string to keep it a good shape while cooking. Melt the butter in a flameproof casserole, add the diced vegetables and set the meat on top. Cover the dish and cook for 30 minutes in pre-set oven.

Pour over the white wine, cover the casserole again, return to the oven and continue cooking to reduce the wine (allow 30 minutes for this). Pour over the stock, which should come half-way up the meat, season, tuck in the bouquet garni by the meat and cover with greaseproof paper and the lid.

Lower the oven to 325°F or Mark 3 and cook the veal for 2 hours.

Meanwhile prepare the soubise, mornay sauce and garnish.

To prepare the soubise : cook the chopped onion gently in the butter until soft but not coloured, add the rice and stock and season. Bring to the boil, cover and cook in the oven for about 30 minutes, until very soft.

Watchpoint You must overcook

rice so that each grain will split. Rub it through a wire strainer or mix to a purée in an electric blender. Then stir in the egg yolk and cream.

To prepare the mornay sauce : melt butter, remove from heat, add the flour and blend in milk, then return to heat and stir until boiling. Cook for 2 minutes cool, then gradually beat in the cheese and cream. Cover with a buttered greaseproof paper to prevent a skin forming.

Trim and wash the mushrooms and cook for 1-2 minutes in ¼ oz butter, salt and pepper and a squeeze of lemon.

Take veal out of oven and keep warm. Strain the stock from the veal in the pan and thicken lightly with the arrowroot mixture. Taste for seasoning before setting aside for gravy.

Carve the meat, spread each slice with the soubise purée and reshape the joint on the serving dish. Spoon over the mornay sauce and brown in the oven at 400°F or Mark 6 for 12-15 minutes. Pour a little of the gravy round the meat and garnish with the mushrooms. Hand round gravy separately. Serve with boiled rice and brussels sprouts.

Note : if making this dish day before for a party, carve, stuff and reshape joint on party day ; after coating with mornay sauce allow 30-40 minutes in the oven at 350°F or Mark 4 for meat to be hot and nicely coloured.

Braised lambs tongues florentine

6 lambs tongues
3 rashers of streaky bacon (unsmoked)
2 onions
2 carrots
1 stick of celery
bouquet garni
6 white peppercorns
½ pint jellied stock (see page 155)

For sauce
1 oz butter
1 shallot, or small onion (finely grated)
1 rounded tablespoon plain flour
¾ pint jellied stock
1 dessertspoon tomato purée
1 glass brown sherry

For serving
spinach creams (see right)
1 lb potatoes (cooked and beaten to a purée with ½ oz butter, 4 tablespoons hot milk, salt and pepper)

Method

Blanch and refresh the tongues, put in pan with enough water to cover, then simmer gently for 1¼-1½ hours. Drain tongues, plunge them into a bowl of cold water and skin them. Trim and cut away the root.

Set oven at 350°F or Mark 4.

Remove the rind from the bacon, stretch each rasher under the blade of a heavy knife and place them at bottom of a flame-proof casserole. Slice the onions, carrots and celery, put in the casserole and cover. Cook over gentle heat for 10-12 minutes or until the bacon starts to brown. Place the tongues on top of the vegetables, add bouquet garni, peppercorns and the ½ pint of stock. Cover the tongues with a double thickness of greaseproof paper and lid and braise for 45 minutes in pre-set oven.

Watchpoint This braising is to give the tongues extra flavour, but they must be quite tender before the process is started, so do not cut the initial stewing time.

To prepare the sauce: melt the butter, add shallot or onion and cook slowly for 2 minutes: stir in the flour and continue cooking until onion and flour are deep brown. Draw pan off the heat, blend in ½ pint of the stock, the tomato purée and sherry; return to the heat and stir until boiling. Then, with the lid half off the pan, simmer gently for 15-20 minutes. Pour in half the remaining stock, skim sauce and reboil; simmer for 5 minutes. Pour rest of stock into sauce, skim again and simmer for a further 5 minutes. Strain, cover and set aside.

Take up tongues, strain off the braising liquid, return it to the pan and boil hard until it is reduced by half. Add the sauce to this liquid, taste for seasoning and boil up together. Return tongues to casserole and keep warm while beating the potato purée and taking up the spinach creams.

To serve: place the potato purée in the serving dish, take up the tongues, slice in half and arrange on top. Turn out the spinach creams and place round the dish. Boil up the sauce and spoon over just enough to coat the tongues and the base of the dish; serve the rest separately in a sauce boat.

Spinach creams

2 lb spinach
$\frac{1}{2}$ oz butter
$\frac{1}{2}$ pint béchamel sauce (see page 152)
2 eggs
salt and pepper
grate of nutmeg

8 dariole moulds

Method

Cook the spinach in a large pan of boiling salted water for 7 minutes; drain, refresh and press between two plates to remove the excess water. In this way the delicate leaves remain whole and unbroken. Carefully lift 8 spinach leaves (16 if they are small) and ūse to line the buttered moulds; sieve the remaining leaves.

Melt the butter, cook slowly to a nutbrown, add the spinach purée and stir over the heat until dry. Add the béchamel sauce and mix well. Draw aside. Beat in the eggs, season well with salt and pepper and a tiny grate of nutmeg.

Spoon the mixture into the prepared moulds, cover with buttered paper or foil and cook au bain-marie in the oven, under the tongues, at 350°F or Mark 4 for 15-20 minutes.

Sweetbreads soubise

1½-2 lb (2-3 pairs) calves, or lambs, sweetbreads
1 onion
1 carrot
1 clove of garlic
1½ oz butter
1 wineglass white wine (optional)
1 wineglass veal, or chicken, stock (see page 155), or 2 wineglasses stock if no wine is used
pinch of chopped, or dried, thyme
1 bayleaf
salt and pepper

For sauce
¾ oz butter
1 rounded tablespoon plain flour
4 tablespoons onion purée (made with 3 large Spanish onions, sliced, blanched and cooked in stock, then drained and puréed)
1-2 tablespoons double cream (optional)

To finish
2 oz button mushrooms (sliced and cooked in butter)
2 oz cooked ham (finely shredded)
grated Gruyère, or Cheddar, cheese

Method

To prepare sweetbreads : soak them for several hours in salted water with 1-2 slices of lemon, or a few drops of vinegar. Then rinse the sweetbreads, put in a pan and cover with water, add salt and another slice of lemon. Bring slowly to the boil, skimming, then drain and rinse quickly. Remove any ducts and any skin which will pull off easily. Press sweetbreads between two flat dishes or trays — with a 2 lb weight on top — until they are quite cold. Slice onion and carrot and crush garlic. Melt the butter in a pan and sauté sweetbreads for about 5 minutes on each side. After turning them, add the vegetables, shake pan gently and continue to sauté.

Pour in the wine and stock and add the thyme and bayleaf. Season, cover and simmer for 20-30 minutes. Remove breads.

Set oven at 400°F or Mark 6.

To prepare sauce : melt the butter, stir in the flour and strain on the liquid from the sweetbreads. Bring to the boil and add the onion purée. Simmer for 2-3 minutes to a coating consistency, then finish with the cream.

Slice calves sweetbreads in 2-3 pieces (leave lambs breads whole) and arrange in an ovenproof dish. Sprinkle the mushrooms and ham on top. Spoon over the sauce, sprinkle well with cheese and brown in pre-set oven.

Serve with boiled rice or creamed potatoes.

Carving and meat management

When good quality meat is so expensive, it is essential to plan your meals in advance, and to make the most of the meat you buy. In order to do this, you should know the different cuts and what they are best used for. In this section we give examples of meat management, with charts showing the most common English and Scottish cuts of beef, lamb and pork.

Learning how to carve correctly — an almost forgotten feature of gracious dining — is another vital aspect of meat management, because an indifferently carved joint is a waste of meat, no matter how carefully planned, prepared and cooked your meal is.

To be a proficient carver calls for experience which is not always easy to get, but much can be learned from studying the anatomy and bone structure of the joint, and by watching an expert when the opportunity arises.

One of the origins of boning and stuffing was to simplify carving so that all that was necessary was an easy slicing movement of the knife, simple enough for a child to do. But in spite of this, meat — especially beef and lamb — is sweeter when cooked on the bone, and there is a real satisfaction in carving a joint properly.

Remember that the knife must always go right down to the bone. In this way you will be able to keep a presentable looking joint even after carving for 3-4 people.

To do the job properly, good sharp knives are essential. These are :

(a) a long broad-bladed knife, often slightly curved. This is suitable for a round of beef such as silverside, rolled ribs or for a pressed tongue

(b) one with a shorter blade for joints on the bone, ie. sirloin or wing rib of beef, leg or shoulder of lamb.

In addition, although not essential, are :

(c) a poultry or game knife, which has a comparatively short blade.

(d) a ham knife, which is long and narrow, and only necessary for whole hams or gammon joints.

All these knives should have a carving fork (with a guard) in correct proportion to the knife. A point to remember is that if too large a knife is used for a small joint, not only is it awkward to handle, but difficult to get a nice looking portion.

Knives may be made of either good quality carbon, or stainless, steel. Both must be kept scrupulously clean, the former by rubbing well with either a cut potato, or a damp cloth dipped in knife powder. Always keep knives keen and sharpen them before use. Special sharpeners are available for stainless steel, and for carbon steel knives a butcher-type steel is best. An oiled stone can be used, but avoid a coarse stone or carborundum for a fine steel knife.

To sharpen carbon steel carving knives there is a technique. If using a steel, hold it slanting upwards in your left hand (if you are right-handed), and, holding the knife in your right hand, draw it rapidly up and down the steel with the knife slanting very slightly inwards. Avoid having too acute an angle or the cutting edge of the knife will have too direct a contact with the steel. To get an idea of the movement, watch your butcher sharpen his knife. Carbon steel kitchen knives can either be sharpened on a steel or on a fine carborundum. Dip the latter in water, and use the same movement as before for sharpening.

An alternative method, and perhaps one more suitable for those not fully experienced, is to draw the knife away from you 10-12 times up the carborundum. Then turn the knife over and draw it down towards you in the same way, always keeping the cutting edge away from you and the knife almost flat on the stone.

Beef

Choice of cuts

A mixture of the best and the cheaper cuts is often a good investment, eg. a piece of **skirt** or **chuck** bought with the tail end of the **sirloin.** As both skirt and chuck have little, if any fat, the tail end gives additional richness. Alternatively, the tail or thin end could be salted, and then cooked gently with onions, carrots and dumplings to make a lunch dish. Or the meat could be steamed for about 2 hours until tender, then pressed and used cold.

A good **frying steak,** or mock fillet, can be made from the 'nut' of meat that lies along the **blade bone.** Ask your butcher to cut this for you ; and then, if you decide to roast it whole, either lard or bard it with pork fat, or wrap it in beef fat.

Alternatively it could be sliced, batted out well and cooked as steak 'à la minute'. Keep it underdone, as it is more tender like that, and pour over noisette butter at the last minute to keep it succulent.

The more coarsely grained and fibrous meat, eg, **top ribs** (Jacob's ladder), **aitchbone** and **topside,** are all better roasted underdone, the two latter being specially suited to spit roasting.

If using top ribs, roast two-thirds to serve hot first, and then cold. Turn the remaining third into a hot pot with kidney, covered by a layer of sliced potatoes which will absorb the fat from the ribs and make a crisp and succulent topping.

Wing rib, which is the start of the hind quarter, is bought according to the number of ribs required, ie. a 1 bone joint is about 3 lb.

Rib roasts (known as **rolled ribs** if taken off the bone) are 4-5 lb upwards. Cut off about half this, fill with a herb stuffing and roast. The other half can be made into a pie or pudding with $\frac{1}{2}$ lb ox kidney.

A 5-6 lb piece of **sirloin,** with the **undercut,** is also an economical buy. The undercut can be removed and used for tournedos, steaks or for a small roast, the meat marbled with fat can be used with a piece of skirt as suggested previously and the top part can be roasted on the bone. This bone can be used to make stock when the joint has been eaten.

Carving beef

Sirloin

To make carving easier, see that the chine bone is sawn through before roasting. This will mean that the full length of the knife can be used without coming in contact with the bone. If at all possible, cut off the chine bone completely before starting to carve.

To carve sirloin with an undercut (or fillet), see the captions and photographs opposite. Give the outside slice to the person who prefers meat well done, together with a slice of the undercut taken from the outside edge.

For sirloin without an undercut, just slice the meat thinly.

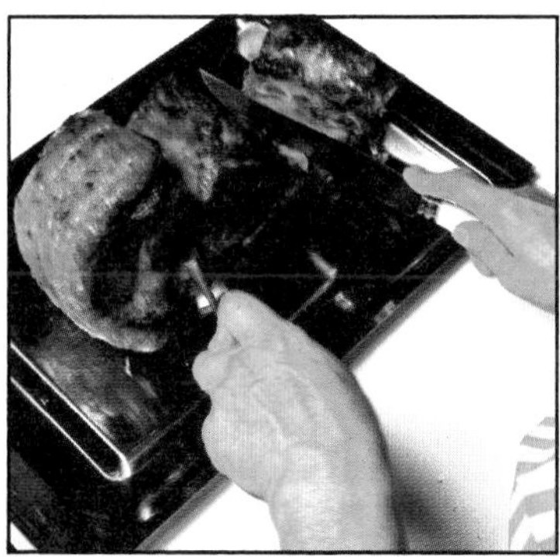

1 *To carve sirloin with an undercut, turn the joint upside down on the dish, ie. on its back. If the butcher has sawn through the chine bone, remove this before starting*

2 *Slice downwards through the undercut to the bone, taking slices not less than $\frac{1}{4}$ inch thick for each person. Continue to carve towards the bone, and as you reach it loosen the meat around it*

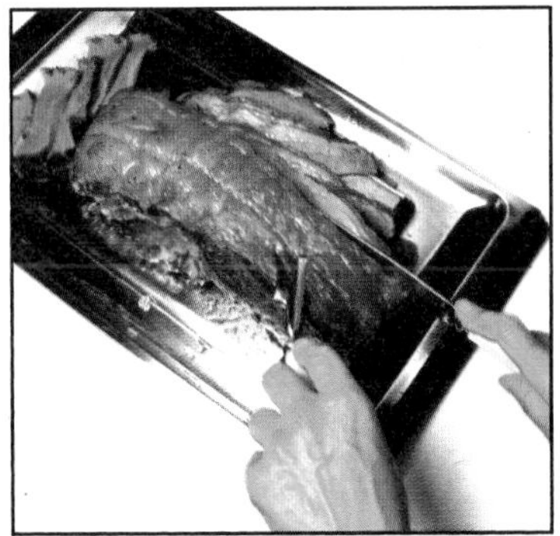

3 *Turn the joint over and slice as thinly as possible down the whole length of the sirloin. Serve each person with a slice of undercut and a slice or two of the top part. Spoon over some of the gravy*

Wing rib

Carve as for sirloin without the undercut.

Fillet

Carve in $\frac{1}{4}$-inch thick slices down to the bone, in the same way as for the undercut on sirloin.

Rounds of beef

Set the meat on the carving dish with the cut sides top and bottom. Insert the fork, with the guard up, into the side of the joint to hold it steady.

Holding the knife horizontally, or slightly slanting, slice thinly from the top right across the grain of the meat.

Beef

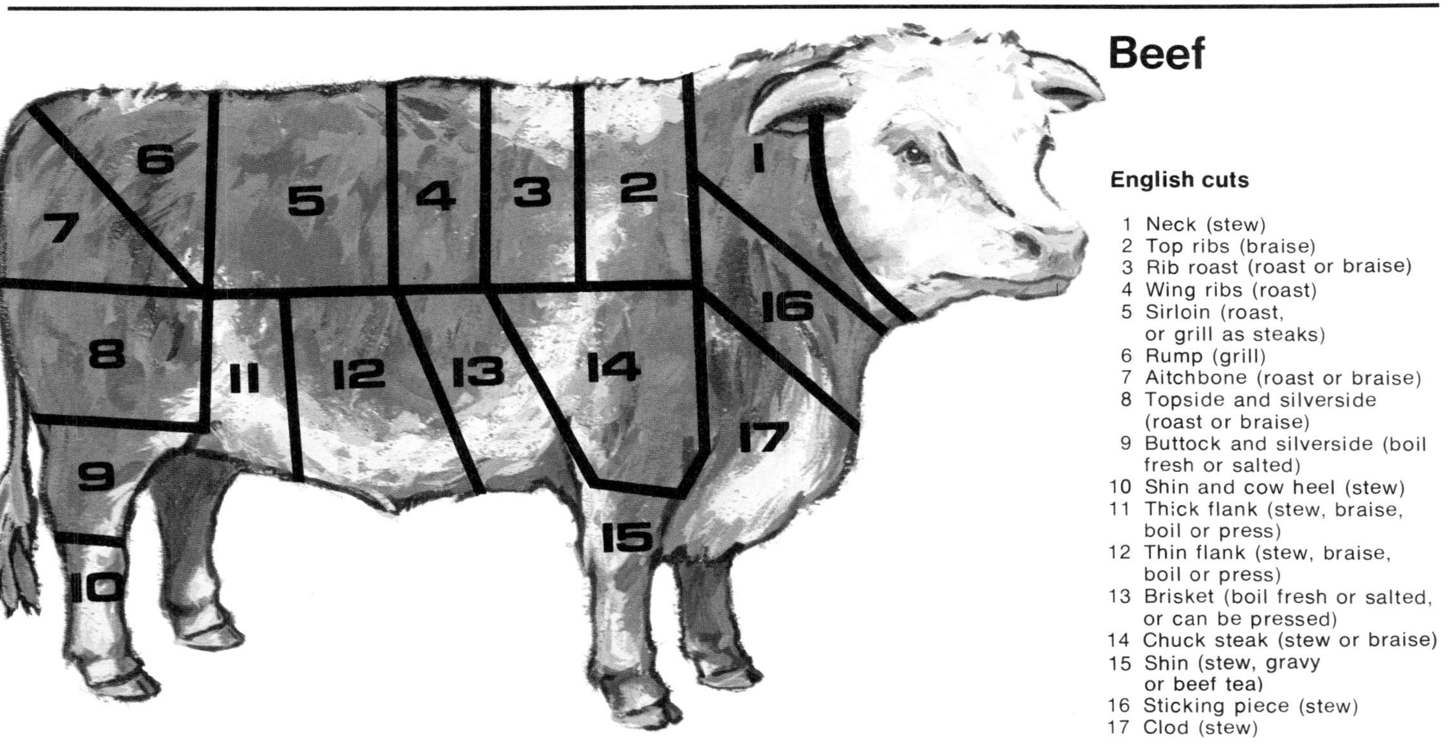

English cuts

1 Neck (stew)
2 Top ribs (braise)
3 Rib roast (roast or braise)
4 Wing ribs (roast)
5 Sirloin (roast, or grill as steaks)
6 Rump (grill)
7 Aitchbone (roast or braise)
8 Topside and silverside (roast or braise)
9 Buttock and silverside (boil fresh or salted)
10 Shin and cow heel (stew)
11 Thick flank (stew, braise, boil or press)
12 Thin flank (stew, braise, boil or press)
13 Brisket (boil fresh or salted, or can be pressed)
14 Chuck steak (stew or braise)
15 Shin (stew, gravy or beef tea)
16 Sticking piece (stew)
17 Clod (stew)

Beef

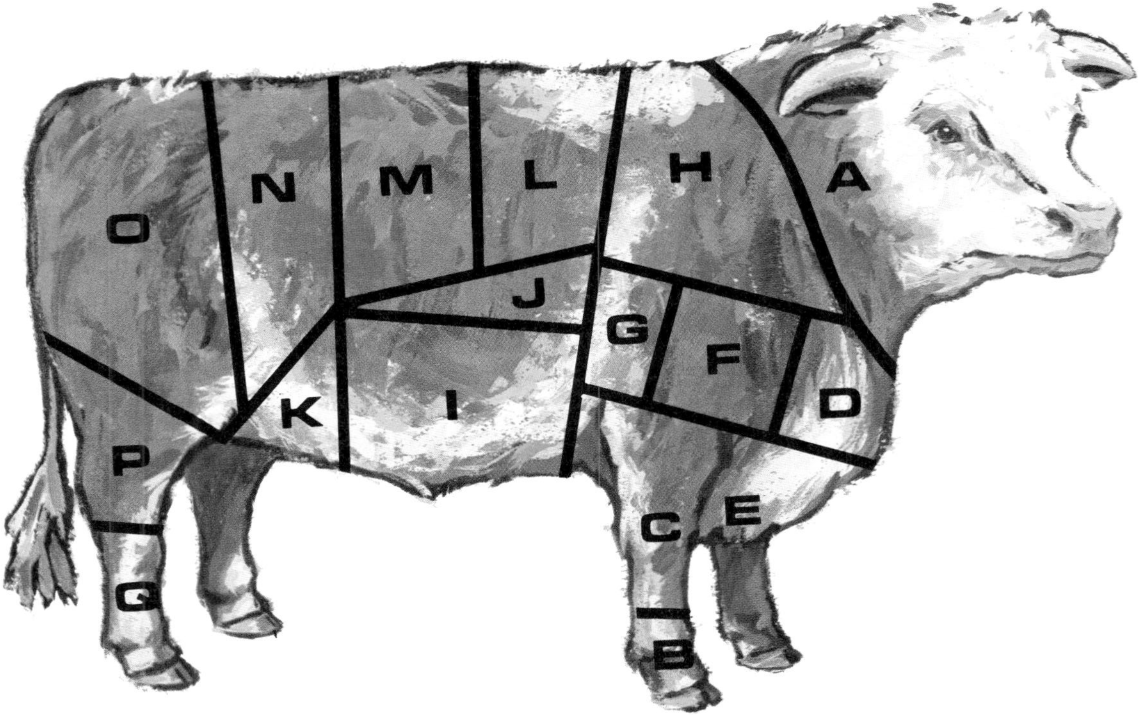

Scottish cuts

- A Neck, or sticking piece (stew)
- B Fore-knap bone (stew, gravy or beef tea)
- C Fore-hough (stew, gravy or beef tea)
- D Gullet (stew)
- E Brisket (boil fresh or salted, or stew)
- F Thick runner (stew or braise)
- G Thin runner (stew or braise)
- H Shoulder (braise)
- I Flank (stew, braise, boil or press)
- J Flank — top ribs (roast or boil)
- K Flank — face of (stew, braise, boil or press)
- L Rib roast (roast)
- M Sirloin roast (roast)
- N Pope's eye (roast, or braise)
- O Rump (roast, braise, or grill as steaks)
- P Hind-hough (braise, or boil fresh or salted)
- Q Hind-nap bone (stew)

Lamb and mutton

Choice of cuts

A joint which gives a variety of dishes is the **fore-quarter.** This consists of the **scrag, middle** and **best end of neck,** and the **shoulder** which may be cut off and roasted. Or, if this is too large a cut, just buy the whole neck. In both cases, the scrag and middle can be used for Irish stew or Scotch broth, or navarin, and the best end for cutlets or a roast.

Another useful cut is a whole **leg** or **gigot.** Choose one weighing 5-6 lb and divide it into three : fillet or top end, middle cut and knuckle. Roast the fillet end — this may be boned and rolled to make a small joint, and the bone used to make a broth with vegetables. The middle cut can form a sauté, and the knuckle can be pot roasted with tomatoes and onions.

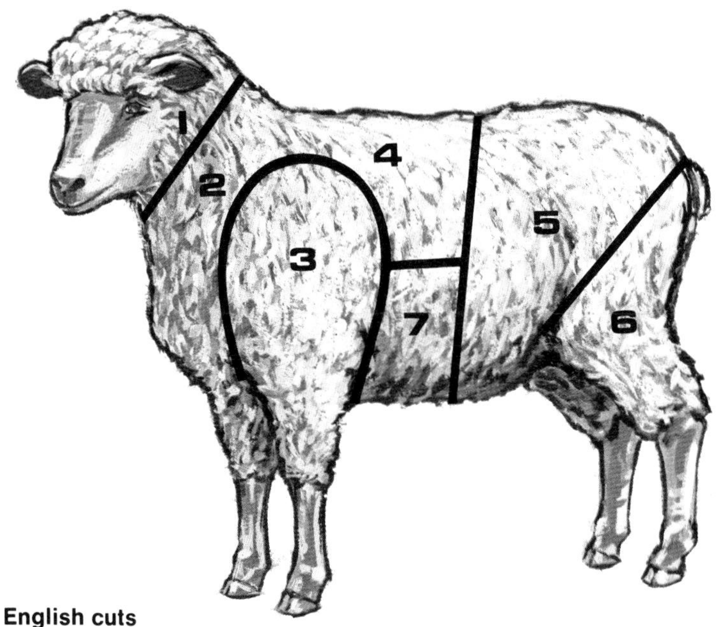

English cuts

1 Head (broths)
2 Scrag (stew)
3 Shoulder (roast or braise)
4 Neck — best end, nearest loin (roast whole or grill as cutlets) — middle neck, nearest scrag (stew)
5 Loin, or saddle (roast or braise)
6 Leg (roast or braise)
7 Breast (stew or braise)

Carving lamb

Saddle

There are two ways of carving saddle. In the first, the slices are carved parallel to the backbone (see photographs 2 & 3 page 144); in the second, which is the easier method if the joint is carved in the kitchen, the slices are cut diagonally or at right-angles to the bone.

For the second method, slide the knife down each side of the backbone (as in photograph 1), then slip it under the meat either side of the bone. Make a cut parallel to the bone about an inch above the dish, and then with the knife held at right-angles, or slightly diagonally to the bone, cut the slices from the bone down the side to the cut line.

Then lift the slices back on to the bone, ready to be served in the dining room.

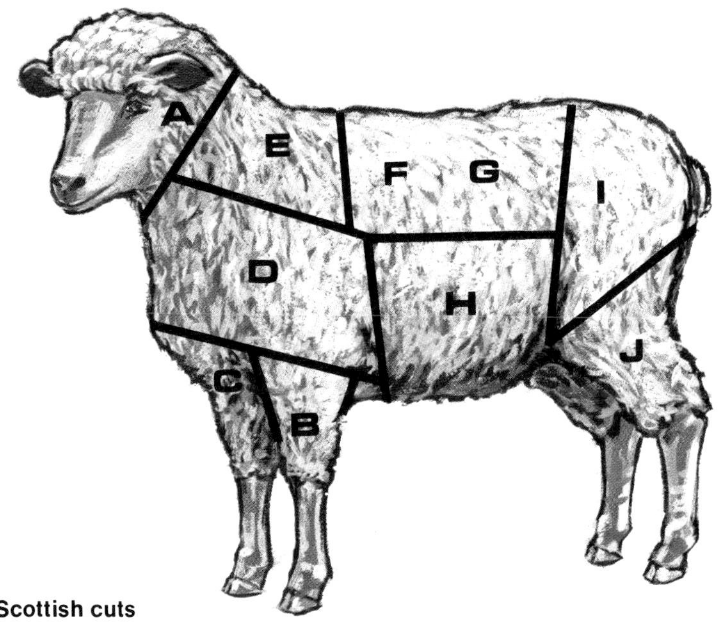

Scottish cuts

A Neck (broths or stew)
B Fore-shank (soups)
C Breast (stew, braise or stuff and roast)
D Shoulder, runner cuts (roast)
E Shoulder, back rib cut (braise, boil or stew)
F Loin, cutlet end (roast whole or grill as cutlets)
G Loin, double loin (roast)
H Flank (roast or braise)
I Gigot, chump end (roast, braise or boil)
J Gigot, shank end (roast, braise or boil)

Lamb and mutton continued

1 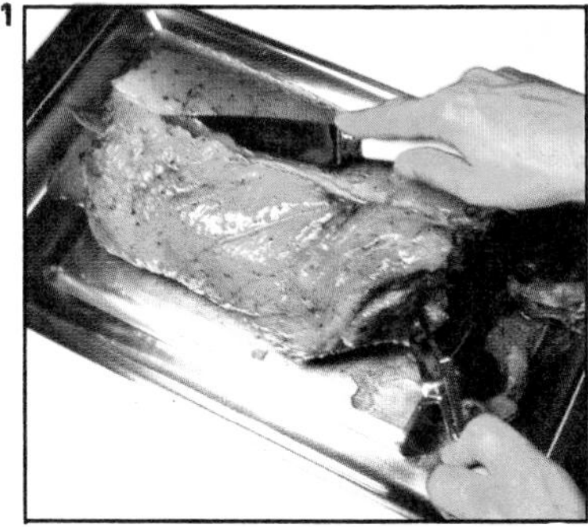

2 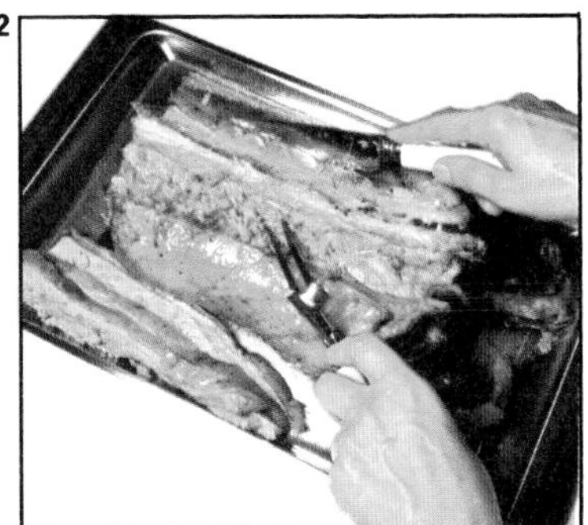

3 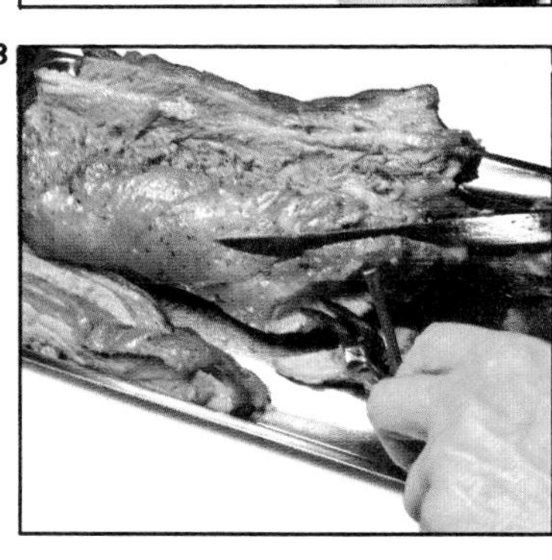

1 *Set the saddle on the carving dish with the tail end towards you. Run the knife down one side of the backbone, and then slip it under the meat which lies on the side of the bone. For more than 4 servings, repeat this on the other side of the bone*

2 *Carve 2-3 wedge-shaped slices down the whole length of each side of the bone, cutting the pieces in half if the saddle is a large one*

3 *Cut slanting slices from the chump end of the saddle and then, for those who like a little fat, cut slanting slices from the crisp flap of the neck end*

Shoulders and legs

Carve both these joints as shown in the photographs and captions 4-8.

To carve a shoulder sucessfully, it is necessary to know where the bone lies in relation to the meat, as this varies according to whether it is a left-hand or a right-hand shoulder (see the diagrams right).

4 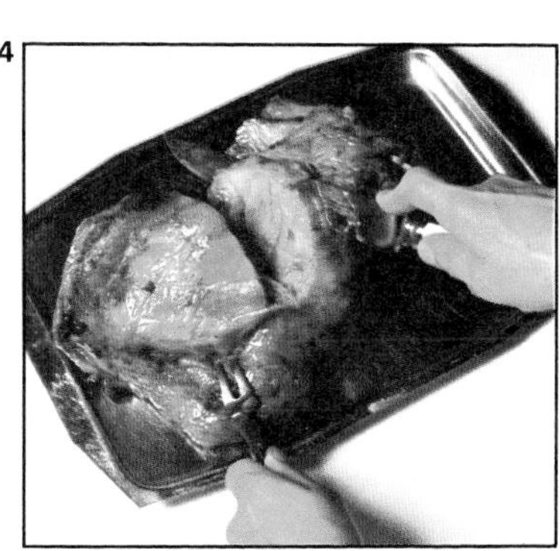

5 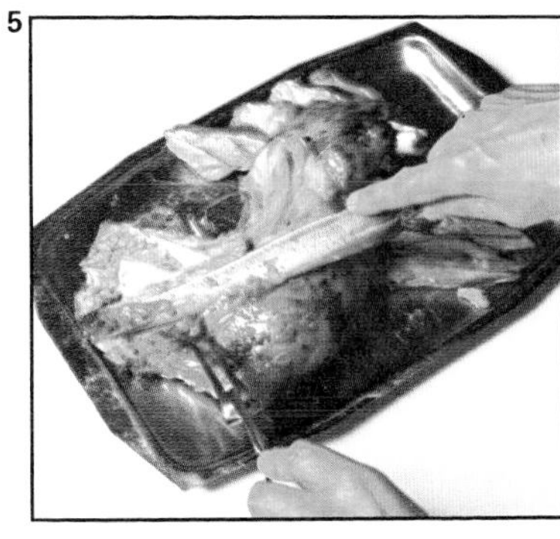

6

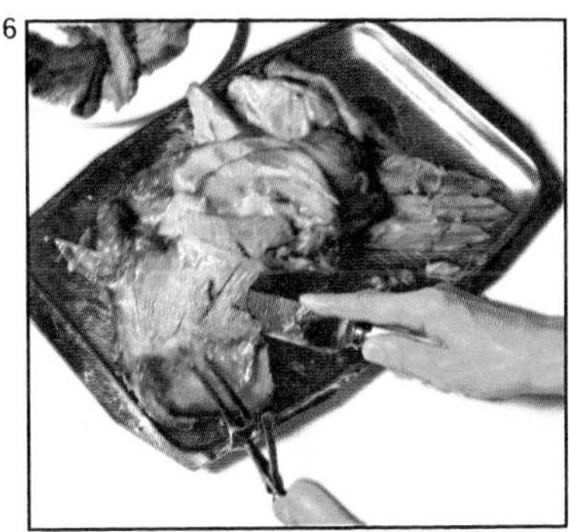

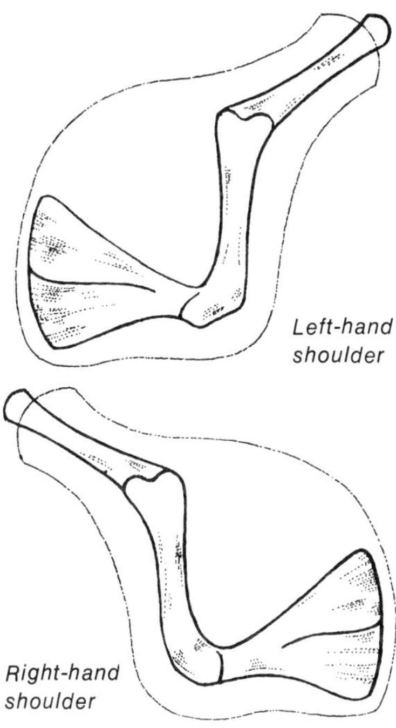

4 Set the shoulder on the serving dish with the meatiest side uppermost and the knuckle away from you (this may be either to the right — as here — or left, see diagrams). Tilt the joint slightly towards you and cut down to the bone in wedge-shaped pieces

5 With the fork, find the spine of the blade bone (the ridge along the top of the bone), and cut wedge-shaped slices lengthwise on either side

6 Turn the joint over and carve thinner pieces from the flat part of the blade bone

7 Set the leg on the carving dish with the round side uppermost and leaning away from you. Insert the fork near the knuckle and tilt the leg slightly towards you to raise it from the dish. Make the first cut diagonally down to the bone. This part has the sweetest meat. Then make another cut ¼ - ½ inch away to give a wedge-shaped slice

8 Continue to carve in this way towards the pelvic bone, slanting the knife as you progress. When this bone is reached, turn the joint over and slice thin pieces sideways and parallel to the leg bone

7

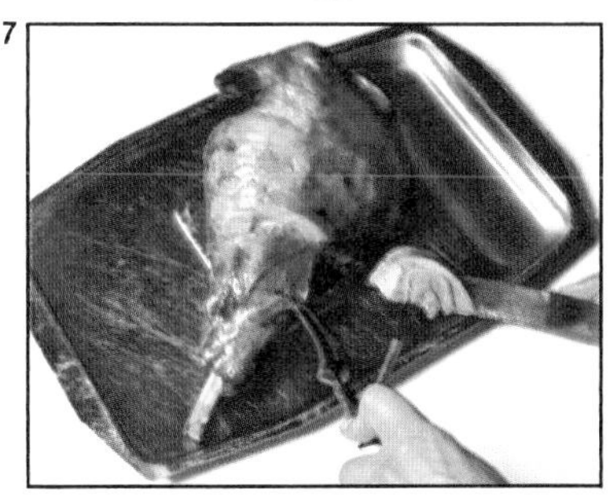

8

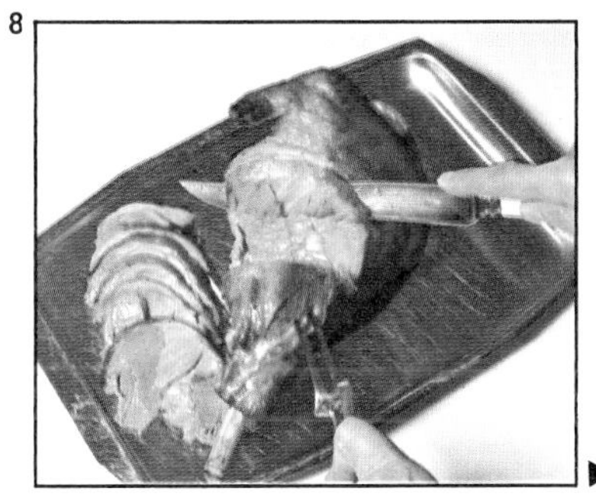

Lamb and mutton continued

Best end of neck

To make something special of a best end, it is worthwhile learning how to prepare a carré d'agneau (see diagrams 1-6), and a crown roast (see diagrams 7-9).

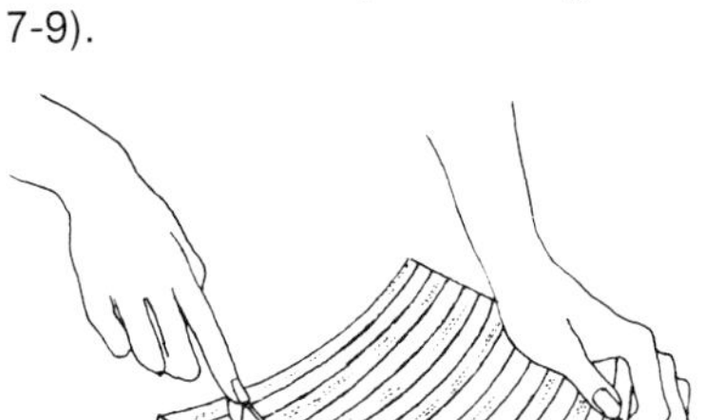

1

2

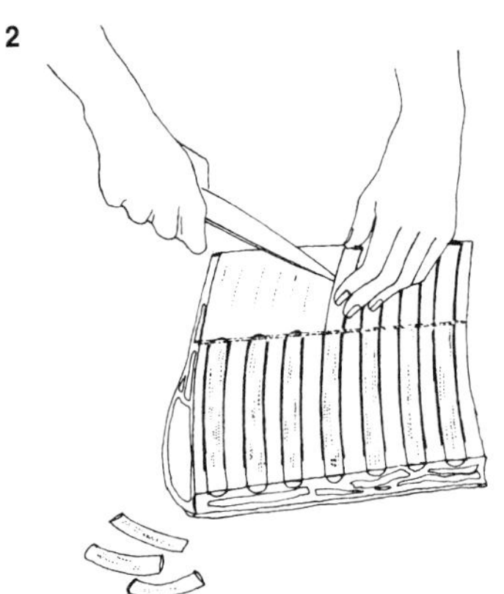

For a carré d'agneau, buy 1 best end of neck (weighing 2 lb) and ask the butcher to chine it and saw a line across the cutlet bones about $2\frac{1}{2}$ inches long, starting from the noix (nut of meat).

1 *Start preparing the joint by removing chine bone (use for gravy).*
2 *Place the joint with the noix furthest away from you. With a sharp knife, and working from the sawn line, cut out and remove the short ends of the cutlet bones*

3 *Cut and loosen the remaining cutlet bones to within $\frac{1}{2}$ inch of the noix, but leave the bones attached*
4 *Make slits through the meat about $2\frac{1}{2}$ inches long, starting from the sawn edge of the bones, by running the blade of the knife along the side of each cutlet bone. Then push the bones through*

3

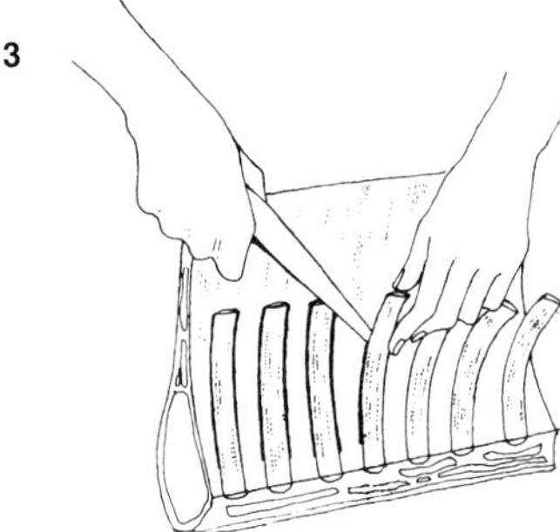

4

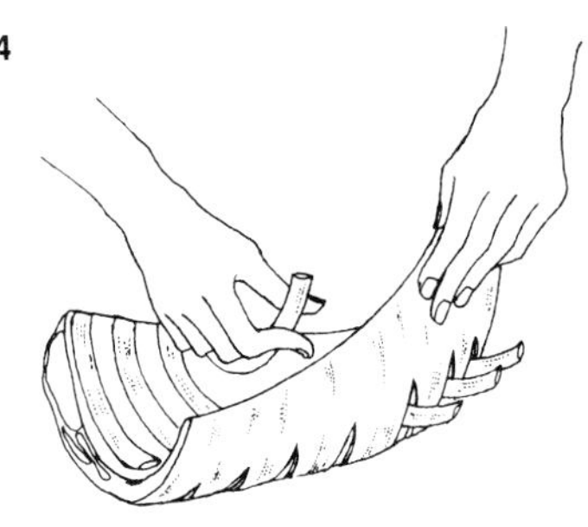

5

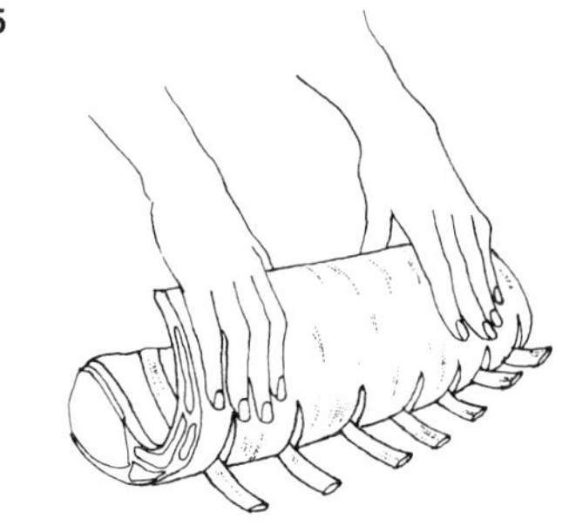

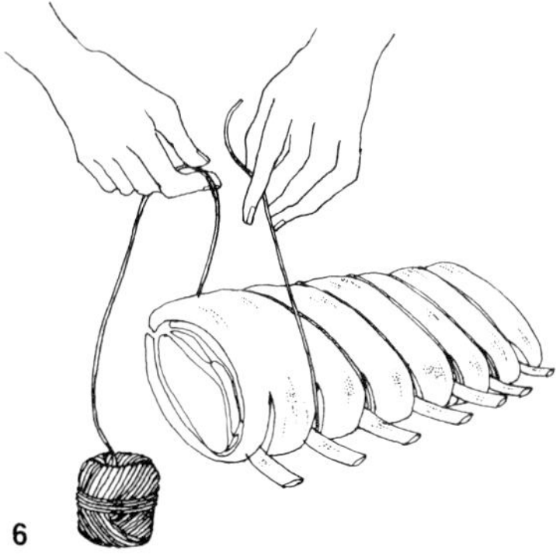

6

5 *Drawing the meat up and back towards the noix, press down firmly so the fatty edges meet (as for a noisette) and the cutlet bones are fully exposed. Cut off a small part of long flat end if this overlaps the noix*

6 *Tie up the joint, bringing the string round the meat in the slits alongside each cutlet bone. To cook: roast as for best end (ie. 20 minutes per lb and 20 minutes over at 375°F or Mark 6 — oven settings are not exactly comparable). Carve by slicing down alongside each bone*

For a crown roast, buy 2 best ends of neck (each weighing 2 lb) and have them chined by the butcher. To prepare, first remove the chine bone.

7

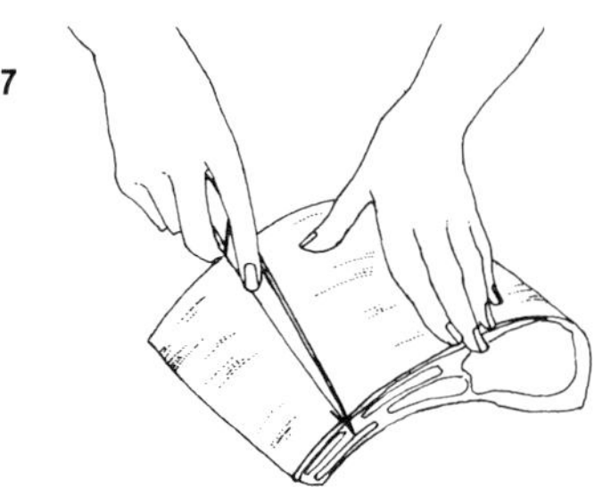

8

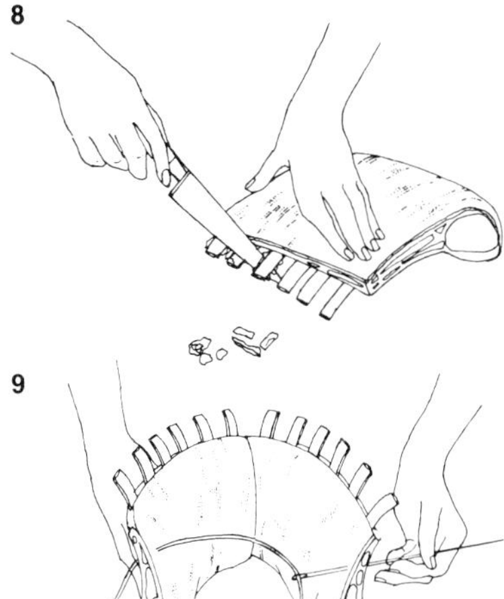

9

7 *With a sharp knife, cut through the flesh an inch or so from the end of cutlet bones on each joint*

8 *Remove the fat and meat from both joints, scraping bones clean*

9 *Using fine string and a trussing needle, sew joints together, back to back (ie. with the fat inside), and with the bones curving outwards. Roast as for best end, basting frequently to ensure the fat is good and crisp*

Pork

Choice of cuts

Gammon is usually the fore leg of pig which has been 'wet cured', ie. in a brine solution. Like bacon (the pig's side which is cured with the leg), gammon may be smoked or unsmoked (green). Ham comes from the hind leg (as can gammon), and is 'dry cured' in a mixture of salt and saltpetre.

A useful pork joint to buy is the **hand and shoulder.** When boned this can weigh about 11 lb or even more, so if this is too much, even for your home freezer, ask the butcher to cut the weight you want.

Use the blade bone end for roasting, and salt the remainder and boil it to serve with pease pudding, or alternatively make it into brawn, augmented by $\frac{1}{2}$ lb shin of beef, if wished.

Buy **gammon** weighing 3-4 lb and braise whole and serve hot with a spinach purée ; or boil, then glaze with sugar in the oven, and serve cold.

Alternatively cut off a third and mince it and mix with about 1 lb minced beef or veal to make a meat loaf to serve hot or cold.

Carving pork

When carving the loin or a piece of the leg with crackling (only these joints have crackling), slice it away first. It can be cut into pieces and put on the dish ready to serve.

Loin should be chined to make carving easier, and leg should be carved in moderately thin slices down to the bone.

Carving ham

Carving a ham in the kitchen is usually done as follows :

Set the ham on the dish or board with the rounded side of the joint away from you as for lamb. Make a cut about 3 inches from the shank bone, first inserting the fork on the near side of the bone right down to the dish or board.

continued on page 52

Shoulder of ham, carved down to the bone in wedge-shaped slices

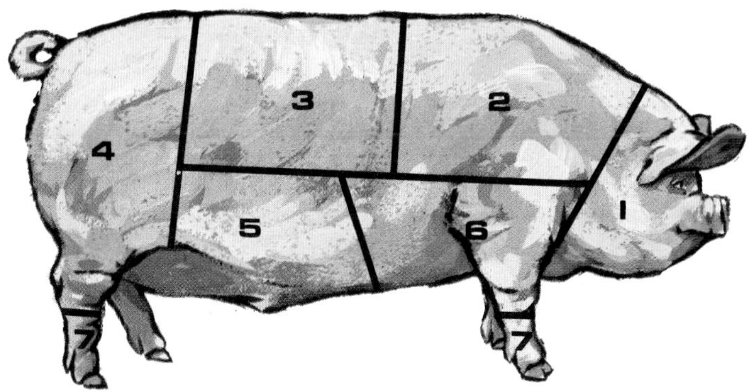

English cuts

1 Head (brawn)
2 Neck, or fore loin (roast or braise)
3 Loin (roast, or grill / fry as chops)
4 Leg (roast or boil)
5 Belly and spring (boil fresh or salted)
6 Hand (roast or boil)
7 Trotters (boil or braise)

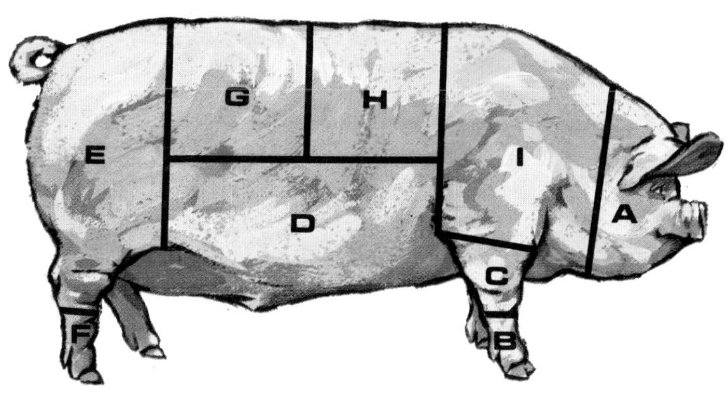

Scottish cuts

A Head (brawn)
B , F Trotter (boil or braise)
C Fore-hough (stock)
D Flank (boil fresh or salted)
E Gigot (roast)
G Loin, double loin (roast, or grill / fry as chops)
H Loin, cutlet (roast, or grill / fry as chops)
I Shoulder (roast, or braise)

Pork continued

Slice the ham in wedge-shaped slices a little less than $\frac{1}{4}$-inch thick, taking the knife right down to the bone and removing first slices as you go.

Continue to slice thinly down to the bone, and after the first 12 or so slices, begin to slant the knife so that when the top bone is reached the knife is almost flat as you carve.

To make the joint tidy again, make sure that the knife goes right down to the bone, and slice off the odd pieces that lie on the far side of the bone.

Carving a ham by the method used in shops and delicatessens involves the use of a ham stand and a ham knife.

The ham is sliced longways, and cut with the grain instead of transversely, as in the first method. Start carving on the rounded side, and allow the knife to travel from the top bone down to the shank, cutting as thin slices as possible.

Appendix

Notes and basic recipes

Béarnaise sauce

3 tablespoons wine vinegar
6 peppercorns
½ bayleaf
1 blade of mace
1 slice of onion
2 egg yolks
salt and pepper
3-4 oz butter (unsalted)
nut of meat glaze, or jelly at base of cake of beef dripping
1 teaspoon tarragon, chervil, and parsley (chopped)
pinch of snipped chives, or grated onion

This quantity is sufficient to put on steaks or cutlets but ingredients should be increased in proportion for a sauce to be served separately.

Method
Put the vinegar, peppercorns, bayleaf, mace and slice of onion into a small pan and boil until reduced to 1 tablespoon. Set pan aside.

Place the yolks in a small basin and beat well with a pinch of salt and a nut of butter. Strain on vinegar mixture and set the bowl on a pan of boiling water, turn off heat and stir until beginning to thicken.

Add the softened butter in small pieces, each about the size of a hazelnut, stirring all the time. Season with pepper. Add the meat glaze, herbs, and chives or grated onion. Keep warm and use as required.

The finished sauce should have consistency of whipped cream.

Béchamel sauce

½ pint milk
1 slice of onion
1 small bayleaf
6 peppercorns
1 blade of mace

For roux
¾ oz butter
1 rounded tablespoon plain flour
salt and pepper

Made on a white roux with flavoured milk added, béchamel can be used as a base for mornay (cheese), soubise (onion), mushroom or egg sauces. Proportions of ingredients may vary in these derivative sauces according to consistency required.

Method
Pour milk into a saucepan, add the flavourings, cover pan and infuse on gentle heat for 5-7 minutes. Strain milk and set it aside. Rinse and wipe out the pan and melt the butter in it. To give a white roux remove from heat before stirring in the flour. The roux must be soft and semi-liquid.

Pour on half of milk through a strainer and blend until smooth using a wooden spoon, then add rest of milk. Season lightly, return to a slow to moderate heat and stir until boiling. Boil for no longer than 2 minutes.

Watchpoint If a flour sauce shows signs of lumps, these can be smoothed out by vigorous stirring or beating with a sauce whisk, provided sauce has not boiled; draw pan aside and stir vigorously. It can then be put back to boil gently for 1-2 minutes before using. If it has boiled and is still lumpy, the only remedy is to strain it.

Breadcrumbs

To make white crumbs: take a large loaf (the best type to use is a sandwich loaf) at least two days old. Cut off the crust and keep to one side. Break up bread into crumbs either by rubbing through a wire sieve or a Mouli sieve, or by working in an electric blender.

Spread crumbs on to a sheet of paper laid on a baking tin and cover with another sheet of paper to keep off any dust. Leave to dry in a warm temperature — the plate rack, or warming drawer, or the top of the oven, or even the airing cupboard, is ideal. The crumbs may take a day or two to dry thoroughly, and they must be crisp before storing. To make them uniformly fine, sift them through a wire bowl strainer.

To make browned crumbs : bake crusts in a slow oven until golden-brown, then crush or grind them through a mincer. Sift crumbs through a wire bowl strainer to make them uniformly fine.

Store all crumbs in a dry, screw top jar.

Demi-glace sauce

3 tablespoons salad oil
1 small onion (finely diced)
1 small carrot (finely diced)
½ stick of celery (finely diced)
1 rounded tablespoon plain flour
1 teaspoon tomato purée
1 tablespoon mushroom peelings (chopped), or 1 mushroom
1 pint well-flavoured brown stock (see page 155)
bouquet garni
salt and pepper

Method

Heat a saucepan, put in the oil and then add diced vegetables (of which there should be no more than 3 tablespoons in all). Lower heat and cook gently until vegetables are on point of changing colour ; an indication of this is when they shrink slightly.

Mix in the flour and brown it slowly, stirring occasionally with a metal spoon and scraping the flour well from the bottom of the pan. When it is a good colour draw pan aside, cool a little, add tomato purée and chopped peelings or mushroom, ¾ pint of cold stock, bouquet garni and seasonings.

Bring to the boil, partially cover pan and cook gently for about 35-40 minutes. Skim off any scum which rises to the surface during this time. Add half the reserved stock, bring again to boil and skim. Simmer for 5 minutes. Add rest of stock, bring to boil and skim again.

Watchpoint Addition of cold stock accelerates rising of scum and so helps to clear the sauce.

Cook for a further 5 minutes, then strain, pressing vegetables gently to extract the juice. Rinse out the pan and return sauce to it. Partially cover and continue to cook gently until syrupy in consistency. It is now ready to be used on its own or as a base for any of the following sauces.

When serving a grill, 1-2 teaspoons of this sauce, added to a gravy or mixed with the juices in the grill pan, makes a great improvement.

French dressing

1 tablespoon vinegar (red or white wine, or tarragon)
½ teaspoon salt
½ teaspoon black pepper (ground from mill)
fresh herbs (chopped — thyme, marjoram, basil or parsley) — optional
3 tablespoons olive oil, or groundnut oil

True French dressing does not have sugar, but for English tastes add a good pinch. When herbs are added to French dressing it is called **vinaigrette.**

Method

Mix vinegar with the seasonings, add oil and when the dressing thickens, taste for correct seasoning. More salt should be added if the dressing is sharp yet oily. Quantities should be in the ratio of 1 part vinegar to 3 parts oil.

Mornay (cheese) sauce

1-1 ½ oz (2-3 rounded tablespoons) grated cheese
½ teaspoon made mustard (French, or English)
½ pint well-seasoned white, or béchamel, sauce

Serve with eggs, fish, chicken and vegetables.

The cheese can be a mixture of Gruyère and Parmesan or a dry Cheddar. If using Gruyère, which thickens sauce, reduce basic roux to ½ oz each butter and flour (1 tablespoon). If too thick, add a little milk.

Method

Make white or béchamel sauce, remove from heat and gradually stir in grated cheese. When well mixed, add mustard. Reheat but do not boil.

Pastry

Flaky pastry

8 oz plain flour
pinch of salt
3 oz butter
3 oz lard
¼ pint ice-cold water (to mix)

Method

Sift the flour with salt into a bowl. Divide the fats into four portions (two of butter, two of lard) ; rub one portion — either lard or butter — into the flour and mix to a firm dough with cold water. The amount of water varies with different flour but an average quantity for 8 oz flour is 4-5 fluid oz (about ¼ pint or 8-10 tablespoons) ; the finer the flour the more water it will absorb.

Knead the dough lightly until smooth, then roll out to an oblong. Put a second portion of fat (not the same kind as first portion rubbed in) in small pieces on to two-thirds of the dough. Fold in three, half turn the dough to bring the open edge towards you and roll out again to an oblong. Put on a third portion of fat in pieces, fold dough in three, wrap in a cloth or polythene bag and leave in a cool place for 15 minutes.

Roll out dough again, put on remaining fat in pieces, fold and roll as before. If pastry looks at all streaky, give one more turn and roll again.

Puff pastry

8 oz plain flour
pinch of salt
8 oz butter
1 teaspoon lemon juice
scant ¼ pint water (ice cold)

Method

Sift flour and salt into a bowl. Rub in a piece of butter the size of a walnut. Add lemon juice to water, make a well in centre of flour and pour in about two-thirds of the liquid. Mix with a palette, or round-bladed, knife. When the dough is beginning to form, add remaining water.

Turn out the dough on to a marble slab, a laminated-plastic work top, or a board, dusted with flour. Knead dough for 2-3 minutes, then roll out to a square about ½-¾ inch thick.

Beat butter, if necessary, to make it pliable and place in centre of dough. Fold this up over butter to enclose it completely (sides and ends over centre like a parcel). Wrap in a cloth or piece of grease-proof paper and put in the refrigerator for 10-15 minutes.

Flour slab or work top, put on

dough, the join facing upwards, and bring rolling pin down on to dough 3-4 times to flatten it slightly.

Now roll out to a rectangle about $\frac{1}{4}$-$\frac{3}{4}$ inch thick. Fold into three, ends to middle, as accurately as possible, if necessary pulling the ends to keep them rectangular. Seal the edges with your hand or rolling pin and turn pastry half round to bring the edge towards you. Roll out again and fold in three (keep a note of the 'turns' given). Set pastry aside in refrigerator for 15 minutes.

Repeat this process, giving a total of 6 turns with a 15-minute rest after each two turns. Then leave in the refrigerator until wanted.

Shortcrust pastry

8 oz plain flour
pinch of salt
4-6 oz butter, margarine, lard or shortening (one of the commercially prepared fats), or a mixture of any two
3-4 tablespoons cold water

Method

Sift the flour with a pinch of salt into a mixing bowl. Cut the fat into the flour with a round-bladed knife and, as soon as the pieces are well coated with flour, rub in with the fingertips until the mixture looks like fine breadcrumbs.

Make a well in the centre, add the water (reserving about 1 tablespoon) and mix quickly with a knife. Press together with the fingers, adding the extra water, if necessary, to give a firm dough.

Turn on to a floured board, knead pastry lightly until smooth. Chill in refrigerator (wrapped in greaseproof paper, a polythene bag or foil) for 30 minutes before using.

Stocks

Brown bone stock

3 lb beef bones (or mixed beef / veal)
2 onions (quartered)
2 carrots (quartered)
1 stick of celery
large bouquet garni
6 peppercorns
3-4 quarts water
salt

6-quart capacity saucepan, or small fish kettle

Method

Wipe bones but do not wash unless unavoidable. Put into a very large pan. Set on gentle heat and leave bones to fry gently for 15-20 minutes. Enough fat will come out from the marrow so do not add any to pan unless bones are very dry.

After 10 minutes add the vegetables, having sliced the celery into 3-4 pieces.

When bones and vegetables are just coloured, add herbs, peppercorns and the water, which should come up two-thirds above level of ingredients. Bring slowly to the boil, skimming occasionally, then half cover pan to allow reduction to take place and simmer 4-5 hours, or until stock tastes strong and good.

Strain off and use bones again for a second boiling. Although this second stock will not be as strong as the first, it is good for soups and gravies. Use the first stock for brown sauces, sautés, casseroles, or where a jellied stock is required. For a strong beef broth, add 1 lb shin of beef to the pot halfway through the cooking.

Chicken stock

This should ideally be made from the giblets (neck, gizzard, heart and feet, if available), but never the liver which imparts a bitter flavour.

This is better kept for making pâté, or sautéd and used as a savoury. Dry fry the giblets with an onion, washed but not peeled, and cut in half. To dry fry, use a thick pan with a lid, with barely enough fat to cover the bottom. Allow the pan to get very hot before putting in the giblets and onion, cook on full heat until lightly coloured. Remove pan from heat before covering with 2 pints of cold water. Add a large pinch of salt, a few peppercorns and a bouquet garni (bayleaf, thyme, parsley) and simmer gently for 1-2 hours. Alternatively, make the stock when you cook the chicken by putting the giblets in the roasting tin around the chicken with the onion and herbs, and use the measured quantity of water.

Vegetable stock

1 lb carrots (quartered)
1 lb onions (quartered)
½ head of celery (quartered)
½ oz butter
3-4 peppercorns
1 teaspoon tomato purée
2 quarts water
salt

Method

Quarter vegetables, brown lightly in the butter in a large pan. Add peppercorns, tomato purée, water and salt. Bring to boil, cover pan and simmer 2 hours or until the stock has a good flavour.

White bone stock

This stock forms a basis for cream sauces, white stews, etc. It is made in the same way as brown bone stock (see page 155), except that bones and vegetables are not browned before the water is added, and veal bones are used. Do not add the vegetables until the bones have come to the boil and the fat has been skimmed off the liquid.

Bouillon cubes

In an emergency a bouillon cube can be used for certain dishes, but it can never replace properly made stock because it will lack the characteristic jellied quality. Bouillon cubes are salty and there is always the danger of overdoing the seasoning.

Glossary

Bain-marie (au) To cook at temperature just below boiling point in a bain-marie (a saucepan standing in a larger pan of simmering water). Used in the preparation of sauces, creams and food liable to spoil if cooked over direct heat. May be carried out in oven or on top of stove.

Baste To spoon hot fat / liquid over food as it roasts.

Blanch To whiten meats and remove strong tastes from vegetables by bringing to the boil from cold water and draining before further cooking. Green vegetables should be put into boiling water and cooked for up to 1 minute.

Bouquet garni A bunch of herbs, traditionally made up of 2-3 parsley stalks, a pinch of thyme and a bayleaf, tied with string if used in liquids which are later strained. Otherwise herbs are tied in a piece of muslin for easy removal before serving the dish.

Butter, clarified Butter which is heated gently until foaming, skimmed well and the clear yellow liquid strained off, leaving the sediment (milk solids) behind.

Croûte Small round of bread, lightly toasted or fried, spread or piled up with a savoury mixture, also used as a garnish. Not to be confused with pie or bread crust (also croûte).

Deglaze To heat stock and / or wine together with flavoursome sediments left in roasting / frying pan so that gravy / sauce is formed. (Remove excess fat first.)

Flameproof Resistant to direct heat as well as oven heat (ie. can be used both on top of the stove and in the oven).

Flour, seasoned Plain flour, to which salt and pepper have been added.

Julienne The cut size and shape of vegetables and garnishes for certain dishes. A julienne strip is usually about $\frac{1}{8}$ inch by $1\frac{1}{2}$-2 inches long.

Liaison Mixture for thickening / binding sauce / gravy / soup, eg. roux, egg yolks and cream, kneaded butter.

Marinate To soak raw meat / game / fish in cooked or raw spiced liquid (marinade) of wine, oil, herbs and vegetables for hours / days before cooking. This softens, tenderises and flavours, and a marinade can be used for final sauce. Use glass / glazed / enamel / stainless steel vessel to withstand effects of acid.

Ovenproof Resistant to oven heat only. Cannot be used on top of the stove.

Reduce To boil down sauce or any liquid to concentrate flavour and thicken the consistency.

Roux Fat and flour liaison (mixture), used as the basis of all flour sauces. The weight of fat should be slightly more than that of flour.

Rust Underside of ham or bacon rasher, on the side opposite the rind. It is often tough and strong flavoured, so should be cut off.

Scald 1 To plunge into boiling water for easy peeling.
2 To heat a liquid, eg. milk, to just under boiling point.

Index